Laura -

take less...

    do more!

Glen Van Perhi

Glen shares my love of road trips and my reverence for the power of wilderness to heal and inspire. **take less. do more.** is packed with tips to get you out into that wilderness with less weight. Glen's book is filled with wisdom on life and how to be the best version of yourself. Working hard to fill up a half-empty world, LOWERCASE-LOVING GLEN invites you to join in.

—**MATTHEW MCCONAUGHEY,** Actor
and *New York Times* Bestselling Author

For the last twenty years, I've studied people who live longer and more fulfilling lives than the rest of the world. Having hiked with Glen, it's no surprise to me that **take less. do more.** contains many tips on the practices evidenced by people in the Blue Zones for a longer and more satisfying life.

—**DAN BUETTNER,** National Geographic Explorer,
#1 *New York Times* Bestselling Author, and
Founder of the Blue Zones.

take less. do more. is not just for the ultralight set. It is a *must*-read for anyone who is looking to expand their capacity to love and give back to others. Although Glen is a legend in the ultralight community, he is so much more than that as a human being. He truly lives by his own philosophy and actually does and gives more than he takes. His words are an antidote and a salve that are critical for our times and will help readers to live fuller and richer lives by taking less.

—**DR. BEN MICHAELIS,** Psychologist, Coach, CEO
of thegroup.io, and Author of *Your Next Big Thing:
10 Small Steps to Get Moving and Get Happy*

My epiphany started with a garage filled with possessions; Glen's was prompted by a backpack that was too heavy. His book **take less. do more.** details his journey to lighten his backpacking load and his realizations along the way of the greater applications to all of life. In it, you will find inspiration to shed stuff, not so you can simply own less, but to help create a life filled with more of what matters.

—**JOSHUA BECKER,** Minimalist, Speaker, and
Bestselling Author of *Things That Matter*

As a backpacker, I mark my years as "BG" and "AG." Before Glen, I thought a boyhood in the woods and a career filming hikes on every continent had given me decent skills, but then came one epic trip with this thru-hiking legend. Now After Glen, I have a whole new philosophy around wants and needs. His book **take less. do more.** will change the way you think about backpacking, and life.

—**BILL WEIR,** CNN Correspondent, host of *The Wonder List,* and Author of *Life as We Know It (Can Be)*

Who knew wisdom weighed so little? In this engaging memoir, engineer and outdoor gear innovator Glen Van Peski takes us on a beautiful journey with his pursuit of the lightest-possible backpack—and the surprisingly deep life revelations discovered along the way. By examining everything we carry—literal backpacks but also metaphorical loads like expectations, clutter, and busy schedules—and focusing only on what's essential, we make room for stronger relationships and richer experiences, proving we all have more to gain by carrying less.

—**HENNA PRYOR,** 2x TEDx and Global Keynote
Speaker and Author of *Good Awkward*

By mastering the art of minimalism, Glen Van Peski wound up with all the things money can't buy: a loving spouse, happiness, deep friendships, an open mind, contentment, calmness, generosity, kindness, a legacy, health, and true freedom. This book helps you stop to consider what constitutes a well-lived life and how you can actually have one. It's simpler than you think.

—**DAVID MCLAIN,** *National Geographic* Photographer

If Glen Van Peski is talking about hiking ... or business ... or life, I'm a listener. **take less. do more.** gives everyone the chance to walk alongside one of the most insightful people I've ever known. His combination of knowledge and experience make him an expert guide on the most challenging trail of all: Life.

—**ALEXANDER GREEN,** *New York Times* Bestselling Author, Chief Investment Strategist of The Oxford Group

I've known Glen since the dawn of the modern-day ultralight backpacking movement. **take less. do more.** details his journey and inspires us to move forward in our own journeys. Glen's generosity and thoughtfulness have had a profound impact on my personal and professional life.

—**RYAN JORDAN,** Founder, Backpacking Light

Glen Van Peski's life spent on the hiking trails of the world taught him to put one foot in front of the other, over and over; never carry unnecessary baggage; remain curious, adventurous, and open; and always know a good water source. But **take less. do more.** ascends to a transformative guide of life, philosophy, and psychology, which promises to lighten our load, keep us steady on the path of life, and help us find our purpose.

—**ALI SELIM,** Director Marvel's *Secret Invasion* and the Spirit Award-winning film *Sweet Land*

With humility and humor, Glen distills wisdom earned from hard nights on the trail and from his extraordinary life. Keeping with his ultralight ethos, his writing is concise, yet chock full of lessons applicable for everyday life, even for folks who never intend to back-pack. For thru-hikers, Glen is one of the fathers of ultralight back-packing and a legend. This book and his life story are testaments to the fact that legends are not born, but built through deliberate thought and persistent practice. Through his storytelling and well-chosen anecdotes, I hope for the world that his life philosophy will become as widespread as his ultralight message has become in back-packing today.

—LIZ "SNORKEL" THOMAS, Award-winning Author, Writer, and Speaker, and Long-distance Hiker.

Glen has walked a different path than I have, but **take less. do more.** reveals a similar passion to mine for getting everyone—especially underrepresented groups—outdoors (and with lighter loads). I have been the personal recipient of Glen's generosity, curiosity, and creative problem-solving, and I recommend this book as a way to walk alongside Glen and learn some of the lessons he's absorbed.

—CRYSTAL GAIL WELCOME, Writer and Backpacker

Glen epitomizes what it means to "leave it better than you found it." In **take less. do more.** you see how he incorporates this in every aspect of his life. In a world where we often don't see nor hear enough about kindness and decency, Glen personifies this and is someone who people of all ages and backgrounds can learn from.

—MATT ABRAMS, The Abrams Group, Advisor, Investor, Cofounder, Board Member

I met Glen deep in Buckskin Gulch and loved his unique concept of "The List" for getting people out into the wilderness. As we connected outside of the canyon, I grew to appreciate his passion for applying his wilderness learnings to all of life. **take less. do more.** shares the stories of how the wilderness taught him lessons in generosity, balance, and curiosity and the importance of relationships.

—**MELISSA WRIGHT,** co-owner of
Women Who Explore

I've known Glen for years, not as an ultralight backpacking legend, but as a down-to-earth engineer and thoughtful business leader. When you dive into **take less. do more.**, you get a view into the Glen I've come to know. His quiet humility, unwavering dedication to his team, and his generosity shine through the stories, offering meaningful lessons for all of us trying to build lives that truly matter.

—**JENNIFER COYLE,** CEO North Star Consulting,
Executive Coach, Speaker

I've hiked with Glen deep into Buckskin Gulch and can attest that he knows more about taking less and doing more than anyone I know. He shares my passion for getting people into the wilderness and removing barriers to make the experiences more accessible. His book **take less. do more.** can certainly help you get out into the wilderness with a lighter load, but also contains many life lessons applicable beyond backpacking.

—**KATHLEEN SCHNEEMAN,** CEO, Explore Austin

Some authors use research and theories to write books. The principles in this book have been tested and consistently lived by my friend Glen Van Peski.

—**DAN ROCKWELL,** Leadership Freak,
Executive Coach, Keynote Speaker

take less. **do more.**

take less. do more.

SURPRISING LIFE LESSONS
IN GENEROSITY, GRATITUDE, AND CURIOSITY
FROM AN ULTRALIGHT BACKPACKER

Glen Van Peski

Founder, Gossamer Gear

Published by Forefront Books, Nashville, Tennessee.
Distributed by Simon & Schuster.

Library of Congress Control Number: 2024900153

Print ISBN: 978-1-63763-289-5
E-book ISBN: 978-1-63763-290-1

Cover Design by Bruce Gore, Gore Studio, Inc.
Interior Design by Bill Kersey, KerseyGraphics

Printed in the United States of America

TO

READ MILLER

AND TO ALL THOSE WHO SEEK

ADVENTURES OUTSIDE IN

WILDERNESS AND INSIDE THEMSELVES.

Contents

"The Legend"

I FIRST MET GLEN VAN PESKI IN THE SUMMER OF 2003, JUST before beginning my thru-hike of the Colorado Trail with two hiking buddies. He visited me at my Boulder, Colorado, summer home. The previous year I had thru-hiked the Appalachian Trail (AT). That is also when I discovered ultralight backpacking. Like Glen, I first awoke to the joys of carrying a really light pack through Ray Jardine. His updated edition of the *Pacific Crest Trail Hiker's Handbook* came out in early 1999 as *Beyond Backpacking*. During the fall of 2001, as I began preparing for hiking the AT, I read everything I could find about this iconic trail and found Ray's book. I read it several times and decided that if I was going to hike all 2,168 miles, I needed to seriously lighten my load.

Back in 2001 that was much easier said than done. Where to find the gear I needed? Back then there were no Z-Packs, Mountain Laurel Designs, Tarptent, or very many of the other amazing ultralight gear companies that exist today. Internet retailing was in its very earliest stages, and Amazon was still only selling books. I did the best I could with the options available to me back then, such as buying a lot of Go-Lite gear. However, I could get my base weight (pack weight not including water, food, or fuel) down to only about twelve pounds. I was really proud of that number twenty years ago.

Little did I know that I would eventually be able to cut that number in half and not give up any comfort, warmth, or safety.

While I didn't know about Glen's company, Gossamer Gear, back in 2001, I discovered it soon after I finished my Appalachian Trail thru-hike and became a customer. I became a disciple of Glen's Ultralight Gospel. I also became a serious gear geek and systematically began thinking about every piece of hiking gear I used, always asking the same question: Can I find something lighter that is just as functional? No gear escaped this ruthless examination, including backpacks, tents, tarps, sleeping bags, bivys, cook systems, puffy jackets, sleeping pads, hiking poles, clothing, shoes, and rain gear. I was and still am looking for better solutions, always testing my personal limits for comfort on the trail versus comfort in camp.

When I met Glen that summer, I met a man I both liked and admired—and someone who was a civil engineer and made his own gear. We talked about gear and hiking for many hours, and I learned an incredible amount from him. I knew this was a guy I wanted in my life. Ever since then, Glen and I have been on dozens of hikes together in many different places around our amazing planet. I am still learning from him every time we are together, and I am deeply grateful to him.

Before Glen left Boulder in 2003, he told me he was going to be forced to shut down Gossamer Gear. He just had way too much going on with work and family to keep it operating. I thought about it for ten seconds and then told him I would buy the company from him. I didn't want Gossamer Gear to cease to exist. It was just too important to die. This sounded pretty good to Glen since he was just going to close it down and receive no money at all. I also didn't have the time to operate this business, since Whole Foods Market took up most of my life energy, so we hired one of my friends, Grant Sible (trail name Gorilla), who had thru-hiked the Appalachian Trail with me and was looking for his next thing to do in life. I convinced Glen to keep 25 percent of the business for himself in exchange for him agreeing to continue to think about our gear and how to make it lighter and better. This proved to be a winning business strategy, and Gorilla did a great job operating and growing the business, while Glen continued coming up with amazing gear innovations. Gossamer Gear steadily grew year after year after year and now has become a highly successful business that we are all very proud of.

Glen truly is a humble guy and a servant leader with a deep care and appreciation for every person his life touches. He is a committed Christian, and if all Christians were like Glen and his amazing wife, Francie, well, probably the entire world would become Christian!

I love the book you hold in your hands. Why?

1. It has a lot of great and interesting stories—stories about his life, his family, working, ultralight hiking, long-distance biking, and many others.

2. There is just enough information on ultralight gear and hiking to stoke people's interest.

3. The book is full of hard-earned wisdom and fantastic advice about how to live a more meaningful, caring, and happy life.

Glen is a firm believer that subtraction rather than addition would serve most people better. He has successfully applied his ultralight principles to the totality of his life and rediscovered a very old philosophical principle: the simple life is a good life. By uncluttering our lives, we can have a more fulfilling existence. Glen's life has less stuff but higher-quality experiences, values, and relationships. Despite many difficult challenges throughout his life, Glen has never given in to despair but instead has used those challenges to learn, grow, and expand more deeply into love.

Almost all of the long-distance hikers I know have been given a "trail name." Mine is Strider. Most of my hiking friends have trail names such as Irish, Cowboy, Gorilla, True, Rocket Man, The Princess, B.S., Cloud 9, Ma, and Bella. When I first met Glen, he told me his hiking name was "Home Made"—no doubt because so much of the gear he used, he made himself. That's not a bad trail name, but it just never rang true for me to who Glen really is on the trail. A few years ago, a better name emerged while on a hiking trip with him—"The Legend." Glen doesn't like it too much, because he doesn't think he deserves such a name. But he is wrong. Glen Van Peski is truly a legend to his friends and to his fellow ultralight hikers. It is a privilege to know him and to hike together with him on the trail and through life.

John "Strider" Mackey
Cofounder and former CEO of Whole Foods Market
Trieste, Italy, October 2023—while hiking with Glen
and a few of our friends on the Alpe Adria Trail

Preface

THIS BOOK HAS BEEN MANY YEARS IN THE MAKING. MY FRIEND John Mackey made the comment on a hike probably ten years ago now, "Glen, you should write a book. . . . I'll write the fore-word." I replied at the time that there were already excellent books on ultralight hiking and that I didn't see what I had to add. In the years that followed, John would continue making his suggestion at some point during every trip we took. His friends gradually joined the refrain, and as explained in the introduction, I eventually got the spark I needed to start the process of writing this book.

I've been working on lightening my pack weight for a long time, so there's no way to capture everything in a book. Chapter 7 does contain a lot of backpacking tips, but the larger focus of the book are the unexpected life lessons on the power of humility, gratitude, perspective, and service that I learned along the way in my fifty-year quest to lower my pack weight.

There have been times in my life when a person has said something that changed the way I thought about myself or the world. With those words, I was able to restore a relationship, achieve a goal that had been eluding me, or incorporate habits and perspective that made me a better version of myself moving forward. It is my hope that for a few people, you might find such words between the covers of this book. For everyone else, I hope my book helps you travel with a lighter pack wherever your journeys take you and that you find encouragement to create a life that's less about having and more about being and doing.

Introduction

IT'S ABOUT A SEVEN-MINUTE WALK TO MY NEW JOB AS A DISH-washer at the amazing Sparrow Bakery in the Northwest Crossing neighborhood of Bend, Oregon. I know it sounds crazy, especially for someone recently retired, but I took a part-time dishwasher job there as a way to connect to my new community. They were having trouble finding someone for the position, and so I thought, *Why not?* The place is always filled with interesting young people and has a great vibe. One of the principles that's guided my life is to step up when or if no one else does, and I feel drawn to the venture. What have I got to lose?

My wife, Francie, and I have been living in this magnificent corner of the Pacific Northwest for less than a year, and the beauty of the place still takes my breath away. As I hike through this delight-fully crisp midmorning, I'm filled with gratitude for the life I'm living. That is another of my core principles: be grateful. We moved here from northern San Diego County after I retired from a four-de-cade career as a civil engineer and she from her career as a NICU nurse. Along the way, I also founded an ultralightweight back-packing company, Gossamer Gear, that's chugging along nicely and generating millions in annual sales—though I never worked for the company full time. And now that I'm retired from civil engineering, I am making different choices on how I spend my days.

Some days, I use my free hours to bone up on languages. Lately, I've been learning French, Italian, German, and Japanese. People always ask if I get bored being newly retired. I've been a very busy and productive person throughout my life, so the question makes sense, but the truth is, I never get bored. I'm eternally curious and always have more interests than I have the time to pursue.

As I make my way down John Fremont Street toward Sparrow Bakery, I zip my Montbell puffy down jacket to my throat, feeling the crispness of the morning nip at my cheeks, though my hands don't need gloves just yet. Winter is almost here. The vibrant fuchsias and violets of summer have faded, and soon the yellow, red, and orange remnants of fall will be gone as well, and an eiderdown of snow will return to the mountains. In some ways, this change of season mirrors my own life. I've moved into the latter stages and I'm really enjoying the view from here. I breathe deeply and inhale notes of ponderosa pines and Douglas fir. Despite living most of my life near the beach, I've always known that I'm really a mountain guy. This move has been good for me. Francie and I are both thriving in Bend.

Some days I work on making new gear for myself, some of which becomes Gossamer Gear products. Will that fabric hold? Will that zipper be able to withstand the pressure? Will my design for a patented cooking system work? I love trying to solve these engineering puzzles; plus there's something about helping others to be lighter in the backcountry that brings me deep satisfaction. My efforts allow others to see more of this amazing world, thanks to the lighter weight they're carrying.

As you will see, the concept of "take less, do more" is not only the official tagline for Gossamer Gear; it has become the primary theme of my life. All the lessons in this book originate in this core breakthrough idea: the less encumbered we are in our lives, the more we are free to do. At least that is what I have discovered in my life. (This even carries over to how Gossamer Gear displays the theme, which is always lowercase since it uses "less" ink.)

On other days in Bend, I go out for fifteen-to-thirty-mile gravel bike rides or ski outings depending on the weather, or maybe I meet new people in our newly adopted hometown, inviting Pacific Crest Trail thru-hikers to stay with us for a night or hosting "Growler Thursdays" for our neighbors. Though I'm definitely an introvert, I push myself out of my comfort zone to connect with those who are both interesting and interested (another principle), people who have something to say but nothing to prove. In between, I manage our rental properties, advise a couple of local start-ups that I have a stake in, volunteer at the city of Bend on their implementation of a new permitting system, and help out friends with land-use issues. I try to stay open and alert to opportunities as they come along, always keeping a keen eye for fun things to do and places where I can add value.

And for me today, that fun thing means something a little different than others might expect: I'll be pulling a six-hour shift washing dishes at Sparrow Bakery. Fulfillment, I've come to realize, is all about what I can add to the stream of life.

By the time I enter the bakery at nine, the place is already rocking and rolling. The line for pastries, lattes, and sandwiches is out the door, and the voices of customers and employees echo in the big industrial space made even more cavernous by its tall ceilings. People come from a hundred miles or more to sample our world-famous Ocean Rolls, a type of buttery croissant dough sprinkled with cardamom, vanilla, and sugar. Those rolls and our cinnamon knots and sandwiches, like our celebrated take on the Monte Cristo, are what have given the bakery its reputation as one of the best breakfast and lunch spots in Bend, a fact that's made clear by the kinetic crowd filling the space.

I say hi to Rilee and my other coworkers as I enter, then duck into the employee area to pull on the cotton apron I wear over my T-shirt and jeans for washing dishes. I change my shoes too. That was the pro tip from coworker Kyle, to keep an old crummy pair of shoes in my locker for work hours to prevent tracking in bakery debris when I return home.

The other dishwashers at Sparrow sometimes prefer the heavy rubber apron when using the big industrial machine in the back corner of the kitchen, but I usually demure. That extra protection is often futile. No matter what I do, I frequently end up with my socks and shoes damp, my fingers wrinkled from the effort. Still, believe it or not, I enjoy myself here.

Though I'm early for my shift today, it's clear from the get-go that my efforts are badly needed. I hup-to, and in no time I've worked through the pile of bowls and pans from the bakers, who have been at it since 3:00 a.m. I bring nine large baking racks to the back, where I soak them with detergent and degreaser; later, I'll chisel away the burnt-on sugar and butter with a bench knife. But first, I need to make sure the front-of-house staff and savory cooks have all the clean plates and mugs they need to keep up with the orders.

At Sparrow, the bakers are the rock stars and the baristas are the artistic geniuses, but without clean dishes, the whole enterprise comes to a screeching halt. Isn't this the way life often is? Everybody has their part to play, and every part is an important note in the overall melody.

I grab tubs of mugs, glasses, and dishes from the eating area as baristas pull shots of espresso and top drinks with steamed milk in the shape of ferns and smiley faces. Bakers craft amazing pastries while the savory cooks assemble hot sandwiches and other treats. By whisking away the dirty dishes and replenishing the food service areas with fresh ones, I contribute to the workings of this well-oiled machine. It's a good feeling to be part of a team.

The first hour passes quickly, then there's a slight lull between breakfast and the lunch crowd. I push a huge tray of dishes and silverware into the industrial machine in the dish corner and pull down the door to start it, my face beaded from the heat and the humidity.

"Hey, Glen," Rilee calls out down the hall from the dining room. Most of my coworkers are twentysomethings and they see me as the somewhat eccentric old guy who has chosen to join them for some inexplicable reason. "When you have a minute, come back out. I want you to meet my mom. She's visiting from California."

Rilee works as a barista and takes orders at the front counter. He's easily distinguishable among all the other young men of Bend by his love of purple: purple fingernails, purple clothing, sometimes even purple hair. Otherwise, he's a fairly typical Bend local—a rock climber and outdoor adventurer, someone who works a job that allows him as much free time as possible to spend in nature, enjoying this magnificent place to its fullest.

Rilee and I became acquaintances before I even started working at Sparrow. When Francie and I first moved here, I came in as a customer and would chat with him and some of the other crew members during down times. He barely scrapes by—nobody's exactly getting rich working here—and when he told me about the demise of his old backpack, I brought him a new one from my collection. I have some extra inventory on hand from Gossamer Gear and I know that practicing generosity with others is a way to fill my own cup (yes, another core principle). Then, when someone gave me a new pair of sandals to test, thinking Gossamer might want to carry them, I asked Rilee his size. The sandals didn't work for me, but Rilee had just been looking for a new pair and they were perfect for him. Since then, we've swapped stories about our adventures and plans, and I've listened to his tales about the crazy parties and out-there expeditions he and his buddies enjoy. In my mid-sixties now, I'm happier listening to those hair-raising stories than joining in. Still, it's one of the reasons I like working here, how my faith in young people today is buttressed with every interaction. Many of my coworkers, some still in high school, are dedicated, hard-working, and passionate about service. Being around them makes me feel good—and hopeful.

I enter the dining room to find Rilee standing next to an attractive middle-aged woman who clearly resembles him. I wipe my hands on my apron and make sure it's centered on my chest before extending my hand in greeting. "Hi, I'm Glen."

"This is Marie, my mom," Rilee says.

Marie and I talk for a moment about living in southern California, sharing some of our favorite haunts. When a line starts up at the door again, Rilee leaves us to resume his place at the counter. I'm about to grab a tub of dishes and head back to the kitchen when Marie stops me.

"Glen, I just want to thank you for helping Rilee. He told me of the pack and sandals you gave him. That was just so kind and generous."

"It was nothing."

She touches my wrist and looks at me intently. "I just hope your backpacking company takes off. Soon." There's a concerned note in her voice. "I have a really good feeling about it. Just hang in there, okay?"

I thank her for her kind words, grab the tub, and head back to the kitchen, ready to prepare another load for the dish machine.

But as I work, her words reverberate in my brain. I'm a little abashed. She clearly came to a conclusion about me that's erroneous, though an entirely reasonable assumption based on appearances. Here I am, a sixty-something-year-old man working as a dishwasher in the bakery where her son is just scraping by. She assumes I'm doing this to keep a roof over my head until my entrepreneurial venture takes off, a tenuous expectation at best. She has no idea that Gossamer Gear is already successful. In fact, Whole Foods Market cofounder John Mackey became my business partner more than a decade ago. Plus, I did well enough with my civil engineering career that I never needed to take a salary from Gossamer. She has the whole story wrong. Oh well.

I stand amid the piles of sticky, dirty baking trays, my arms wet with soap, and am amused to find myself here on this beautiful morning. My life has taken some odd meanders, for sure, and I wouldn't change a thing. Yet people often ask me what's my secret for contentment, and now I have to wonder myself what it is. I take a kind of inventory on how and why I'm here washing dishes, and in that moment, a new thought begins to take form. It's as if bread crumbs of thoughts lead me from one place to another.

I realize that back in the day, when I focused on reducing my backpacking weight, the innovations I developed, small as they were, created ripples for countless thousands of backpackers hoping to do the same. To be honest, though, that hadn't been my intention. Really, I'd only wanted to lighten my own backpacking load, and yet in doing so and in offering what I discovered freely to others, I helped many people lighten their own loads as well and thus helped them better enjoy their trips in the wilderness. I'm proud of that fact.

The philosophy that guided my ultralight backpacking innovations—"take less, do more"—also guided me in just about every aspect of my life, and really, it is what has brought me here to Sparrow today. This approach has helped me find a way to give back to my community, to be part of a team, a worker among workers. This philosophy has applications for anyone regardless of age, career status, and income level wanting to live a more rewarding life.

I use the industrial-strength sprayer to wash off flecks of pastries and bread crusts from plates, stacking coffee mugs in the trays as an even bigger idea clicks into place. Maybe, just like helping others reduce their backpacking weight, I've developed ideas on living a deeply satisfying life—one that encompasses humility, service, and gratitude—that might be of interest to others, even those outside the backpacking community.

It's often said that if you want to really master something, you need to teach it. When I was newer in the ultralight backpacking space, I'd get together with others, and after a rigorous outing together, we'd unpack our individual packs to see the choices each of us had made and how our unique selections had worked out. It was a way of learning from our community and calibrating anew each time how to get closer to the ideal we were each shooting for. Sharing our experiences with each other—both the failures and successes—sometimes helps to illuminate our individual paths.

There in the dish corner with my hands all soggy and my face beaded with steam, a flash of inspiration hits me. That's what I should do now. I will unpack all I've learned along the way, both about how taking less into the wilderness allows us to do more but also, even deeper, how applying this philosophy in just about every area of life can make for a richness of experience that's available to anyone who wants it. This philosophy has become a cornerstone in my life, and perhaps it's time for me to give it away.

I'll start jotting down ideas as soon as I get home, but first, I have a shift to finish. I pull down the door to start a new load of dishes and head back to the dining room to grab another tub.

take less

The Wilderness Provides Perspective

It was 2019 and we were gathered in the Café Rio, a popular fast-casual restaurant chain that serves Mexican cuisine in Saint George, Utah, filling our bellies with beans and rice before what was sure to be an astonishing adventure. The group of backpackers I'd organized was about to enter Buckskin Gulch in Southern Utah, a bucket-list-worthy destination for hikers and canyoneers alike. Located in the Paria Canyon-Vermillion Cliffs Wilderness, this three-day outing was part of my philosophy of taking trips with people who don't know each other.

Every year I do this trip and sometimes others, inviting along folks I don't know well. Usually it's people I've bumped into at speaking engagements or interacted with online relating to gear, but sometimes it'll be neighbors or someone I ran into at the grocery store. Sometimes people suggest others who would be good to include, and they get an invitation. This is my way of expanding my own social circle and also encouraging people to get to know others outside their regular lives. Many times, the people who said yes to my invite were relatively accomplished in their professional lives. It's not unusual to have corporate CEOs hiking next to artists who live in obscurity, mixing cheek by jowl with academics who tend toward niche interests. And that's what makes it so enjoyable, having a mish-mash of different ages, experiences, socioeconomic statuses, you name it. There are just so many people we can learn from, and yet we tend to stick with those we already know. This is a way to shake all that up.

For this trip there would be eight of us, the typical eclectic mix, though a little different than usual. Typically I'm the common denominator, the only person everyone in the group knows. This trip had started with an invite to my friend Dan Buettner, a National Geographic explorer, Guinness World Records holder, best-selling author, and creator of the Blue Zones project. Dan said he was in for the trip, then asked if he could bring a friend. A week later he called about bringing another friend. (Dan has a lot of friends.) Finally, I just told Dan that I would make this year's trip for his friends, and he could invite up to six of them. So for this trip, Dan was the common denominator. Among his friends on this trip would be a National Geographic photographer, an award-winning screenwriter, a longtime CNN correspondent, a hotel entrepreneur, and an actor. For my typical trips, the groups tend to include both genders, but for Dan's group, it ended up being all guys.

The outing I had planned was both spectacular and challenging. Permits are hard to come by, and thus few people have had the opportunity to experience the amazing terrain. We would be hiking through an area of Arizona's Buckskin Gulch, which feeds into the Paria River and in turn joins the Colorado River southwest of the Glen Canyon Dam a ways below where we would land.

Buckskin Gulch is known to be—hmmm . . . how shall I say this?—an interesting outing. It's one of the world's longest slot canyons at fifteen miles long and among the deepest at five hundred feet deep. At times, it gets as narrow as two feet across. The water pools in the canyon are often at subfreezing temperatures, flash flooding is possible, and you can quickly sink into quicksand to your thighs. It's on the list of the ten most dangerous hikes in the United States.

Picture it: walls of sandstone surrounding you, virtually insurmountable, as high as a skyscraper as you walk your way down deeper into the skinny, sand-coated (or mud-caked) canyon bottom, farther with each step into what looks to be the depths of the earth, a frigid creek surrounding your ankles. Soon, you're wading through icy water waist high, carrying your pack over your head in the deepest sections, with no escape route except for a sketchy one up a canyon wall about eight miles in. By the second day, we'd end up in a more open area as the river broadened out—much less claustrophobic but with cliffs still looming more than fifteen hundred feet high on either side.

Why do it?

Well, the undulating sandstone walls surrounding you are absolutely breathtaking, showcasing layers of sediment in shades of buff, dried-blood red, earthy browns, and mustard, colors that give insight into the erosion that created this splendor. As you hike through Buckskin, it looks as if you're about to hit a dead end several times. There's seemingly no way through; surely it's not possible to keep going. And then, off to one side, an arch-like space suddenly appears and shows you the way, as if you or one in your group has said the magic words, "Open, sesame." It's nothing short of extraordinary.

And then there's the light.

As you walk deeper into Buckskin, the walls forming those jaw-dropping vistas change colors and shadings depending on the time of day and the angle of the sun that filters through the overhead crevices. That play of sun and shadow is unique to Buckskin and must be experienced to be believed. It's a kaleidoscopic adventure for the eyes. In the early spring, the new leaves on the trees in the canyon look like they're almost glowing green. One year a participant explained to me that the cones in our eyes are each tuned to specific light wavelengths corresponding to red, green, and blue. With all the red in the rocks towering above you, the cones get overwhelmed and the green, by contrast, really pops visually.

Despite all the beauty, though, hikers need to be prepared for the challenging conditions the route presents and be aware of how the weather can turn the hike deadly.

In March 2023, two men died there and eleven other hikers were airlifted out of the vicinity. Admittedly, that was due to the unusual atmospheric river conditions that hammered the area that year. When we were going, in 2019, the conditions were much more friendly, though still nothing to be toyed with.

Prior to this outing, I'd been in communication with all the backpackers, making sure they were on board with going as lightweight as possible, in good hiking shape, and ready for what we were about to do. I gave out advice freely, but I also expected each to be in charge of his own gear and food. I approached the outing like all the rest I'd done.

I have found that being in the wild is a great leveler. No matter who people are in the regular world, when you are walking in the wilderness, perhaps putting yourself at risk, those social or cultural parts of our identities slip away. Nature focuses our attention and makes us narrow our perspective to what is really important— shelter, food, water, and safety. That is when I have space to be able to see more clearly and get perspective. It is also when I am free to take in the beauty and majesty all around me.

This is foundational to my ultralight backpacking philosophy: to have perspective on our lives, to see clearly what is truly needed, and to pack light so we are free to do more.

My "great leveler" philosophy was going to be tested on this hike. It wasn't until I stopped by the Las Vegas airport, picking up the actor member of our group on my way to St. George, that I realized this trip might be a little different from previous excursions.

Sure, I knew the name and well-known face of Oscar-winning actor Matthew McConaughey, who'd be joining us. And I looked at him as I had Dan's other friends, as just another hiker, another human who wanted to experience this rich landscape with us. Unlike with the others, though, I had curated Matthew's gear for him. He didn't have the time to solve the ins and outs of ultralight-weight backpacking, and his handlers knew so little about what we'd be doing that they'd likely be useless. So I offered to handle it and gathered the various gear and specialized clothing he would need for the trip from my personal collection.

Instead of picking him up at baggage claim, I was given instructions to find him at the end of a hidden airport corridor that opened to a side parking lot. It all felt rather mysterious and cloaked in intrigue. Due to his fame, he would be escorted through the airport along that concealed passageway. Maybe I had been too quick to think he'd be like the rest of us. I hoped I wasn't going to be sorry I had told Dan to just invite his friends.

We finally met and he jumped into my Subaru, and when he asked me to pull over on the shoulder of Interstate 15 so he could take a leak, my concerns that he might be a prima donna faded fast. Just in our drive to Café Rio, it became clear he wasn't overly self-focused. He peppered me with questions about the light-weight gear we'd be using, where we were going, who was going to join us, about my life. He was engaged and interested. That was a good sign. As I would come to learn over the next few days with the other men, he's a born storyteller, but he didn't always have to be the one talking. And while he was clearly comfortable being the center of attention, he didn't *need* to be in the spotlight. This was going to work out well.

At Café Rio, though, I could observe the effect he had on other people from the get-go. It was pretty wild to watch.

Matthew came out of the restroom, drying his hands on his pants before extending one to the others in the group, saying, "Hey! McConaughey."

As our group sat down to eat, you could see the furtive looks and elbowing from the other customers in the space. You could almost hear them thinking to themselves and commenting to their neighbors, "Hey, that guy looks *exactly* like Matthew McConaughey. But it can't be, right? I mean, maybe if this was a fancy restaurant in Hollywood or New York City, but at a Café Rio in St. George, Utah?"

I have been around semi-famous people before but had never experienced anything quite like this.

As we got ready to make our way to the trailhead, I went over the gear with Matthew and told him it would make me personally very uncomfortable to head out on a hike where someone else had put together all my gear.

"Well, Glen," he intoned in his classic drawl, "I figure you know a helluva lot more about this than I do, so I'm sure whatever you've assembled will be a lot better than I could have come up with on my own."

I handed each hiker their WAG bags, a waste allevia-tion-and-gelling system, kind of like a doggie poop bag for people. The celebrity in our midst would have to use these just like the rest of us.

We each shouldered our packs and strolled the first easy steps along a dry riverbed, learning about each other, being friendly. I prepared the others for what was ahead, noting that thankfully no rain was in the forecast within a fifty-mile radius. That was a good thing because even a storm a distance away could create a hundred-foot-high wall of water barreling through the gulch, moving as fast as nine feet per second. If it were to rain heavily while we were out in the Buckskin portion of our adventure, we'd risk death—not so much from drowning but from being slammed side to side in the canyon along with uprooted trees and boulders.

As we prepared to wade through a series of puddles left over from the last storm, I explained the water's source. "When rain hits, this little stream in Buckskin Gulch can swell from barely a trickle to more than eight thousand cubic feet per second," I said, and while that wasn't going to happen to us now, it was that periodic rushing wall of water over eons that had sculpted the amazing canyon walls. Those floods, though, dissipated as quickly as they developed, leaving the icy, murky puddles of indeterminate depth that we would be navigating for the rest of the day.

Soon, our feet were numb from the cold water, but our spirits were high. We helped each other down a ladder that had been erected in the gulch to help bridge the sudden drop we were about to traverse. We took turns holding each other's packs, guiding each other with our words and encouragement, spotting each other in case of a fall.

IF IT WERE TO RAIN HEAVILY WHILE WE WERE OUT IN THE BUCKSKIN PORTION OF OUR ADVENTURE, WE'D RISK DEATH— NOT SO MUCH FROM DROWNING BUT FROM BEING SLAMMED SIDE TO SIDE IN THE CANYON ALONG WITH UPROOTED TREES AND BOULDERS.

The first night, some in the group were surprised I hadn't supplied them with proper tents. While two of the guys had brought one-man tents, and one had a piece of plastic he planned to use to keep him dry if it rained, the rest of us would be doing what backpackers call "cowboy camping." And on that first night, it worked well.

But on the second night, gentle rain started to fall. So much for my lecture about how we'd be dry this entire time! Thank goodness we were now camping on the broader banks of the Paria River, no longer worried about possible flashfloods in the skinny confines of Buckskin. Still, I was prepared for this change of weather, carrying an extra-wide piece of plastic in case I needed to cover some of my charges. Two of them, including Matthew, would need this help.

"You'll have to sleep side by side," I told the two guys as they rigged the single piece of plastic with their trekking poles to keep them covered.

Ali Selim, award-winning director of the Marvel movie *Secret Invasion*, would be sharing the makeshift shelter with Matthew and was abashed.

"I wake myself from the volume of my own snoring," he explained. "That's why I positioned myself so far from the group last night."

I had flashbacks to a cross-country bicycle trek in my youth when snoring had caused our group to split up. But there wasn't much we could do about that now.

Matthew, though, was unfazed. "That's okay. I have a technique," he said.

None of us knew what that cryptic statement meant, but we were weary from hiking all day. We'd covered more than sixteen miles trudging through water, over debris and rocks, carrying our packs. We all just wanted to sleep.

The night grew dark and quiet, the moon a fingernail clipping in the sky, the stars a scatter of gold dust against the blackness of night. When, hours later, Matthew's bedmate snored loudly, Matthew put his technique to work, flicking Ali's Adam's apple with his finger, twice. Miraculously, it worked. Both were soon back asleep, as were the rest of us.

Of all the things I thought I might learn from a celebrity on this trip, how to silence a snorer had never made it onto the list.

The next day, we passed a few hikers. We hadn't seen many throughout the excursion. The route is lightly traveled and not for the faint of heart. But each time we did, the same effect I'd noted in Café Rio took place. Hikers looked over their shoulders after we'd passed, staring at Matthew's back as he receded down that trail.

"Couldn't be, could it?" they had to be asking one another. Even half a mile after we'd passed, they were still craning back, trying to discern if that was really Matthew McConaughey they'd just said "Hey" to in the middle of nowhere. Many, I think, thought it was his backpacking doppelganger. Still, the canyon itself did not seem to notice.

On the last day, when walking beneath towering cliffs of Navajo Sandstone in the Paria, walls so high that you can't even capture them in a photo, I felt again what I came to the wilderness to feel: perspective. In much of our life we can seem pretty large in our own eyes. And for someone like Matthew, who's told all the time just how special and unique he is, who cannot walk into a fast-food restaurant without being gawked at, it must have been especially nice. Because, out here, we all saw that we really were not that special.

On the final day, we hiked our way to the end of the canyon close to nightfall. At the parking lot, Ali offered to take our eight WAG bags to the disposal spot.

A hiker from another group followed him on his way to the dumpster. "Hey, give me McConaughey's," he said.

The wilderness, I realized in that moment, was the great leveler. Though Matthew enjoys a degree of privilege few of us will ever fully understand, and one that some of us crave, once we got in the canyon, he had to wade through the mud, sleep in the sand, and poop in a bag just like everyone else.

The experience also taught me that we never know who we're going to meet on our travels—maybe not Matthew McConaughey, but someone almost as interesting, someone you might form a connection with, perhaps someone who can help you with a problem you're trying to solve, or, better yet, someone *you* can help.

By talking with people we encounter in our day-to-day outings, even for an introvert like me—or writing them a note, when circumstances permit—I've ended up with lifelong friendships. Chance encounters can introduce us to our next best friend, to someone who may grace our lives for a day, a season, or a lifetime. But we have to be open to them.

When the trip was over, I took back the gear I'd loaned Matthew, including the sleeping bag he'd slept in. I shipped that off to the dry cleaners as I aired out the packs, hung up my warm puffy, and put away the trekking poles. Our friend Rose came for dinner the following week, and when I told her about the trip with Matthew, she was blown away. I hadn't realized that she was a massive fan of his, and she wanted to hear every detail possible.

What had he ordered at Café Rio? What did he talk about? Was he as cute in person as he was on the screen?

After dinner, she sat on the couch poring through the photo book that the National Geographic photographer had assembled from the trip photos, noting McConaughey in my blue puffy jacket in the group photo. Suddenly I had an idea. Wordlessly, I went upstairs and retrieved my blue puffy. I took it back down to Rose.

"This is the jacket that McConaughey wore in that photo," I said. "In fact, he was the last person to wear this jacket."

She put it on, grinning from ear to ear. I let her take a photo of herself wearing the blue puffy, holding the group photo showing McConaughey wearing that same jacket. She had to promise not to post the photo anywhere, but I'm pretty sure that made her day, or possibly her year.

The wilderness is indeed a great leveler, showing us that we are each a human being trying to get by. But then again, no one was ever so excited to wear a jacket just because *I'd* used it, nor has anyone wanted to claim my WAG bag. I guess celebrities come with a few extra perks.

Take More, Do Less

BEFORE I LEARNED THE CORE LESSON OF MY LIFE—TAKE LESS, do more—I first had to experience its opposite, which I was able to do thanks to my son being a Boy Scout.

Francie sewed the patches onto a pair of tan short-sleeved button-down shirts: troop number, council strip patch, the quality unit award. My version of the shirt differed from my son's only in size. Brian, our oldest who was then eleven, had recently crossed the bridge from Cub Scout to Boy Scout, and I decided to join the troop as one of the leaders.

Before then, around 1996, I'd been working seventy-plus hours a week as a civil engineer, keeping the family afloat—a prospect made especially challenging given the needs of our profoundly disabled middle son, Derek. Between my demanding career, our three children, Derek's unique needs, and the myriad complications that came with all of the above, I realized that for most of Brian's upbringing, I'd been at work, leaving Francie to handle things at home. It was time, I decided, to be more present in his day-to-day life. What better way than joining the Boy Scouts as one of their leaders?

Standing in front of the bathroom mirror, Brian and I each tried on our new shirts, paired with khaki slacks cinched with our official Scout olive green belt.

"What do you think?" I asked my son, less than half my height and a fraction of my weight as we stood next to each other.

"Not too shabby, Dad." He seemed glad I was getting involved, and my heart swelled at having the opportunity to share this stage of development with him. I added the Smokey Bear–type leader hat I'd also bought to complement my uniform and smiled at my son in the mirror.

WE DREAMED OF BACKPACKING LIKE TRUE ADVENTURERS, OF PACKING UP ALL WE'D NEED INTO ONE TIDY COMPARTMENT AND HOISTING IT ON OUR WILLING BACKS, READY TO FEND FOR OURSELVES IN THE GREAT OUTDOORS,

"You're not really going to wear that thing, are you?" he asked, ribbing me.

When I was a teenager, I'd lived with my mother and siblings in Amherst, Massachusetts, while our father stayed behind in the San Fernando Valley of California after the divorce. Though he was a well-versed outdoorsman and had taught me much when I was younger, he hadn't been around during big swaths of my teen years to instruct me on the nuances I missed, nor to prod along my developing maturity as a young man. I loved visiting him over the summers and got much out of that time we shared, but it wasn't the same as having him nearby year-round.

When I was younger, before my parents divorced, we'd done a lot of car camping as a family, loading up into my dad's International Harvester truck and heading out to a national park. Dad was super handy and had constructed wooden drawers in the back of the truck that fit all our gear: camp stove, lantern, and so on. We had one of those old Coleman lanterns, and I loved the mystery of putting a new mantle on. You had to first burn the mantle, then the remaining ash served as the filament on which the gas would burn. Watching it illuminate the night out of its former existence, now just ash, always enchanted me. During quiet moments, Dad would rummage for the perfect piece of pine firewood and whittle it into something astonishing and miraculous. Once, he created a ball inside a cage, connected via a chain—all carved from a single piece of wood.

I have limited memories of those trips, but I do remember being amazed by the Steller's jays common in the Sierra and how they were able to identify raisins pictured on our Sun-Maid boxes. If we left a box out, they'd go to town pecking at the sweet dried fruit until they'd filled themselves to the point of gluttony.

By the time I was a Boy Scout myself, about Brian's age, though, I was living on the East Coast, far from my father, and my Scout experiences were less than magical. We pitched our tents for over-nighters at the local campsites in the nearby woods on the weekends, but we didn't do any real backpacking per se. I don't think we ever ventured into the backcountry. Though I owned and treasured a Kelty external frame backpack, it didn't get much wilderness use. I was interested in something more immersive than those local over-night experiences and wondered when I'd ever get the chance.

On free weekends, my buddies and I would ride our bikes down to the local Eastern Mountain Sports store in Hadley, three miles away. Once there, we wandered the aisles, touching the sleeping bag fabrics and trying on backpacks, assessing the gear on offer, spending hours debating the merits of the various Swiss army knives (Victorinox vs. Wenger) and white gasoline backpacking stoves (Svea vs. Optimus). We dreamed of backpacking like true adventurers, of packing up all we'd need into one tidy compartment and hoisting it on our willing backs, ready to fend for ourselves in the great outdoors. anxious to prove we were worthy and strong, ingenious and hardworking, smart and cunning enough to survive in the wilderness. It was many years later before I got that chance.

Brian and I pulled off of El Camino Real into the parking lot of the First Presbyterian Church, which hosted Troop 752, and made our way into the large community room. He took off to meet his friends, leaving me standing in the hullabaloo that swelled all around me. Eventually, I recognized a familiar face.

"Mr. Miller," I said, taking hold of the Scoutmaster's hand in a hearty shake. "Good to see you, my friend."

"Mr. Van Peski," he replied, slapping me on the back. "Welcome aboard."

Our voices were nearly drowned out by the roar of a hundred boys wrestling with each other, sharing notes on Game Boy moves, and generally just horsing around with all the testosterone surges common to young boys turning into men.

I'd gotten to know Scoutmaster Read Miller a few years earlier when we'd both been in Toastmasters working on our communication and leadership skills. He'd also been a client of the engineering firm I worked for, Browne & Vogt, and brought us occasional development projects. We'd enjoyed each other's company. Between working with Read and spending crucial developmental time with Brian, this was going to be fun. Truly, though, I had no idea of the countless benefits I'd eventually reap from this experience and the circumstances that would flow from my involvement.

Our meetings were held weekly on Thursday nights right after dinner—we didn't want to mess with having to offer nearly a hundred boys snacks every week—and included a color guard presentation and the formal aspects of scouting before we broke into groups so the boys could work on the skills they needed to earn merit badges.

Occasionally, we did award ceremonies. We had a huge number of boys on our hands and we held pretty tight rein to avoid pandemonium. The only way to get stuff done was for the adults to take charge, and so that's what we did.

Unlike the troop I'd belonged to as a teen, this one had an extensive schedule with all kinds of outdoor activities—canoe trips, summer camp, you name it—capped off with a weeklong backpacking trip in California's Sierra mountains every year. That's the activity that appealed to me the most, and soon I found myself named Assistant Scoutmaster and the person heading up the backpacking program. I couldn't have been more excited.

Because the boys varied by age, size, and abilities, we decided to create two tracks for those interested in backpacking. Track A would be for the older, more experienced boys and B for those younger, smaller, or newer to backpacking and not quite ready for a weeklong trek in the High Sierra. Each track would undertake three-to-five smaller trips over the course of the year as training. The B track would allow the younger, smaller boys to gain experience and skills on a not-too-difficult level so that by the time they reached Track A, they'd be ready to go, prepared to embark on weeklong, completely unsupported trips into the High Sierra. Now we're talking.

That was the plan. But first, we had to start from ground zero and build that program. The logistics of planning upward of eight separate backpacking trips was daunting.

I stood next to Brian in the aisle of REI and fingered the various internal frame backpacks, remembering my days as a young teen with my buddies in Eastern Mountain Sports. A lot had changed since I'd bought my Kelty external frame pack in Massachusetts, and I was fascinated by the advances. But which backpack would be best? Which felt good on my shoulders? What did I truly need? As I weighed these questions, Brian dragged over compasses, water bottles, and backpacking stoves for me to examine. He was giddy with the thought that we could get what we needed, and though I played up my engineer persona, looking at each item's functionality through a dispassionate lens, the teen boy who'd wanted to buy everything at Eastern Mountain Sports was doing a happy dance inside.

Though I'd done a cross-country bicycle trek when I was younger, it had been a long time since I'd immersed myself in a wilderness-type setting in which I had to carry everything I'd need. I had a lot to learn.

I looked over the equipment list Read and I had developed and began ticking items off. Both Brian and I would need backpacks, sleeping bags, and sleeping pads. I'd carry the tent, stove, cooking kit, water filtration system, and dinners in my pack to give Brian's young shoulders a break. The aisles surrounding us, meanwhile, were crammed with headlamps and lanterns, packable camp chairs, portable showers, coffee presses, fancy pots and pans. What was truly a necessity? Would we be glad for a little added comfort on the trail, like that extra plush sleeping mat? Did we really need a bear canister?

Eventually, a saleswoman came over to help us and in no time sorted out what she considered to be the bare minimum that we'd need. Brian and I each picked out heavy-duty boots, the old-fashioned leather kind that we'd need to spend some time breaking in. We each tried ours out on the little rock in the store to see how they'd feel on a descent. I spent a bundle that day at REI, and that was without buying any of the fancy extras. We could always add those luxuries later if we found we really needed them.

At home, Brian and I unpacked our purchases and spread them across the living room floor, determined to figure out how everything operated and how we'd organize all this gear into our packs. Grant, our youngest son, now nine, looked on with Francie. Neither seemed to understand what all the excitement was about.

Brian and I set up our tent in the backyard, practiced inflating our sleeping pads, and debated how much clothing to take. When it was getting close to time to leave on our first-ever backpack outing together, I made the mistake of weighing my fully loaded pack. It tipped the scales at 71.5 pounds. Wow. That was heavier than I was expecting. But I was in my forties and strong enough. How hard could it be? Brian's pack, thankfully, came in closer to 40 pounds, but still, that was a lot to ask a thirteen-year-old to carry. Still, that's what this experience was all about, wasn't it—testing our limits, understanding that perhaps we were stronger than we thought we were? Either way, I knew we'd manage. We spent some time breaking in our boots and then were ready to head out.

WE TOOK OFF FROM THE TRAILHEAD ON OUR WEEKLONG OUTING WITH ALL THE JOY AND ENTHUSIASM OF TRAILBLAZERS OF OLD, EIGHT YOUNG BOYS AND FOUR LEADERS.

With a series of training hikes under our belt, that fall we drove up to the Sierra for the true test of our conditioning. We took off from the trailhead on our weeklong outing with all the joy and enthusiasm of trailblazers of old, eight young boys and four leaders, including my buddy Mr. Miller, on this inaugural expedition for Brian and me.

We weren't going to discover any new territory or name a new peak, but we had the zeal of those who would. Laughter and high spirits surrounded us. We were leaving everything behind for a week and about to have the time of our lives.

For the first day, we planned to do ten to twelve miles. That goal had seemed perfectly reasonable sitting around the dining room table at a planning session. Even if we went at a pace of only one and a half miles an hour, super slow, we'd get to our first planned camping spot with daylight to spare. As we hiked on, the trail snaking uphill, switch-back after switchback, the excitement of the morning died down and the boys got quieter. They still noticed lizards crossing the trail and marveled at an eagle overhead, but their vocal enthusiasm lessened with each step as the reality of what they'd signed up for hit home.

A mile or two in, the weight we carried combined with the ascent started to take a toll, even on me. I was able to manage the weight; I'm a big guy and could handle it, but frankly I was grateful Brian wasn't carrying any more than his forty pounds. By now, a number of the boys were lagging. Read and I tried to keep the boys' spirits up and hopeful. "Look at that beautiful pine tree!" "Did you hear that chickadee call just a moment ago?" "Check out this amazing wildflower!"

They went along with it, but the weight of what they carried was pulling their spirts down.

By day two on this expedition, the weather had grown merci-lessly hot, and we were ascending some tall passes. Plus there were mosquitos. That night, we made camp at Silver Lake, right near a big mountain pass we'd conquer the next day. Everyone dropped their packs with audible relief as we started to orga-nize dinner. The mosquitos, I noticed, were bad, likely due to our proximity to the lake. I put a mosquito-net head cover on as I cooked and ended up spooning mouthfuls of dinner to feed myself from underneath the head net. Not all the boys wanted to wear their head nets, and they were getting eaten alive. Even going to the bathroom was hard because the minute you pulled your pants down, the mosquitos swarmed the uncovered flesh. It was not pretty.

By the evening of day three, we were all dragging, so much so that the sun was going down long before we made it to camp. I debated in my head whether we should turn around the next day and try to go back or just continue on, but the cars were at the trail-head we were moving toward, and I knew we'd eventually be okay. As we hiked, I could see tears welling in Brian's eyes even in the scant illumination of twilight. It was getting on toward full dark. The boys were hungry and weary. I moved my position to be at the back of the line of boys so that Brian wouldn't have me nearby to see him in his misery. I wanted him to have a chance to gather himself. Besides, I worried: *Had we pushed them too hard? Why were we all struggling?*

I realized that planning hiking mileage while you're sitting around a kitchen table with a map, nice and comfortable, is one thing, but getting on the trail is another. Some of the kids were not in the greatest shape, many carrying extra pounds on their bodies that made the hiking hard. We'd occasionally had trouble finding water, and one boy had sprained an ankle. Things go wrong; that's the nature of the beast, I told myself, but this was maybe too much.

By the time we made it to camp that night, Brian's tears had ceased but we could see that all the kids were beat and at the end of their ropes. We hung our food from a tree after dinner to keep it safe from bears and then all bedded down for some much-needed rest.

In the middle of the night, though, we heard commotion. In the beam of a flashlight, we saw a bear cub, sent by its mom, scrambling up the tree to retrieve our food. We started making noise, as we'd been instructed to do, creating pandemonium in the middle of the night. We managed to scare the cub away but could see bears just beyond our little gathering, waiting in the darkness for us to doze off again so they could strike. We'd be in deep trouble with these boys if we managed to lose our food to those hungry bears, so that night we built a couple of perimeter fires, and the other leaders and I took turns keeping watch; no one got much sleep.

The ridiculous part was the next morning. We got the boys up— they'd all gotten some rest, thank goodness—and started hiking again. We weren't a mile down the path when what did we run into? A bear box! We could have just locked up our food there and been spared such a difficult night, but this was before GPS and detailed information on such things on the internet.

It was in that moment that I realized all I'd been given by signing up to be a Boy Scout volunteer. Sure, there was a lot of shared suffering on the trip, but what memories Brian and I were making with each other. We'd never forget this, and so many of these boys would go on to become leaders in their own ways because of this experience. I was overcome with a sense of gratitude: How lucky I was to be here! How much I had to be thankful for.

Still, the trip wasn't over. Though the boys were pretty ragged by this point, they kept moving forward. They were being good sports considering they'd had to navigate quite a few miserable moments. But that's the great thing about backpacking. You have to keep hiking to get through the difficult patches. No matter what, you can't quit. In a way, it's great training for life. When we give of what we have (our time, our talents, our resources), the dividends that return to us are seldom what we think they're going to be, and in my experience, they are always—always—much greater than I could have wished for.

That trip, for instance, in addition to creating memories with my son and maybe inspiring some boys to recognize their deep inner strength, sparked ideas in my head about gear. If we'd been carrying less, if we'd thought through some of our gear choices in greater detail, perhaps there would have been more moments of rapture at the beauty of the mountains and less preoccupation with our misery. Maybe there was a better, more efficient way to do this—a way that would have made the trip even more enjoyable and memorable for everyone.

It wasn't the first time I'd had such thoughts.

Lighten Your Load

WE WERE SITTING AROUND A SCATTERING OF OUTDOOR TABLES at In-N-Out Burger in San Bernardino—Read Miller, me, a few other Scout leaders, and about a dozen boys who'd just walked their feet off over the last seven days. Everyone had aching shoulders and backs, abraded hip bones, and bruised clavicles, but as we sat down to our first not-in-the-wilderness meal in a week, the pain and misery we'd just endured seemed to evaporate.

The boys stole fries from one another, scarfed down Double-Doubles as fast as they could cram them into their mouths, slurped shakes loudly, and joked with each other. The outing had definitely included plenty of suffering along the way, but wasn't that just another way of saying it had been a golden opportunity for "character building"? Shared endurance of hardships, after all, makes for very good friends.

The boys told and retold the story of the bears and rattlesnakes we'd seen and evaded, while Read and I quietly remembered how we'd almost lost one kid over a waterfall. We'd been crossing a stream, something we were always very cautious about. We'd strung a rope across the waterway and attached it to trees on each side so the kids had something to hold on to as they waded through. The bigger Scouts wore their packs on their backs but unbuckled their waist belts so if they fell and their pack filled with water, they could quickly shed the pack before being dragged under. With the younger boys, we set up a Leader Shuttle to ferry their packs to the other side so they only had to get their bodies across the creek that rushed past our feet, frigid with ice melt. Just beneath where we were attempting this crossing, a waterfall churned and convulsed, reminding us of the danger. If a kid slipped, it would take only a moment before he'd plunge into the waterfall's giant agitator.

I stood in the middle of the freezing creek, just making sure each kid got across safely. It all was going well when one younger, slight boy, Kevin, slipped and fell. Thank goodness my instincts were sharp. I grabbed him just in time and basically threw him to the far bank, my heart hammering like a timpani. We'd narrowly avoided a very serious accident. The boys hadn't realized how harrowing that moment had been, especially not Kevin, and I wasn't about to tell them. Read and I counted our lucky stars.

But now we had warm burgers in our bellies, and the work and danger were all behind us. We felt good. After two hours in the car, we'd all be back home and heading toward our warm, soft beds and the most delicious moment of any backpacking trip—the first hot shower post-expedition.

As Read and I finished our burgers and shooed the boys to clear their tables, he mentioned a book he'd been reading, *The Pacific Crest Trail Hiker's Handbook* by Ray Jardine. "I'd like to do the PCT, in sections," Read said. "But the only way I'll survive is by reducing the amount I'm carrying. This business of moving so slowly because we're lugging so much won't get me there."

"What?" I asked, feigning surprise. "You think seventy pounds is a lot?" We'd both talked until we were blue in the face that there had to be a better way to do this, to see more of the wilderness while not breaking our backs, but we really didn't know where to begin.

"The guy in the book, he gets his base pack weight down to something like eight pounds," Read marveled as we shepherded the kids into the cars for the ride home. "You think we could do that?"

"Eight pounds? That's crazy! Still, if we *could* get that light, imagine how much easier it would be, how much farther we could travel." My mind spun with possibilities. The seed had been planted.

When I got home, after enjoying a good night's sleep, unpacking all the gear, and nursing my feet and shoulders back to health, I got a copy of the book and totally geeked out. The author included gear lists (my favorite thing), and I got to work weighing absolutely everything I took on a typical backpacking trip to understand what I was up against. I asked myself a series of hard questions: Did I really need extra pairs of underwear? Was there a more lightweight way to cover myself in the event of rain than the typical rain gear I lugged? Was a tent truly necessary?

A revolutionary change was unfolding in my brain as I went through and reconsidered all the received "wisdom" I'd acquired around backpacking. I put every edict I'd learned about backpacking under a microscope and began examining and tinkering with what I found.

I started with the internal frame backpack I'd bought at REI, hailed as the best option for the type of backpacking I was doing, given five stars by just about all the experts. The pack, though, completely empty, weighed a whopping seven and a half pounds. Seven and a half pounds of nothing except a hollow container! There were so many places I could direct my lightening-the-load focus— my sleeping bag, the clothes I packed, my stove, my air mattress, how much water I carried. If I scattered my attention that way, though, I feared I would soon be overwhelmed, and so I started with what seemed the most egregious waste of weight: the pack itself. If I could significantly cut down on that fundamental piece of gear, I'd be making good progress.

I remembered the 1976 cross-country bike trek adventure I took with my friends after high school and thought back to all the ideas on traveling lighter that had started germinating in my brain. Now I was ready to put them to work. I'm an engineer by training, and solving this kind of puzzle has always been one of my favorite pastimes. I knew there had to be a better way to venture into the wilderness, but what was it exactly?

My mom was a big believer in making sure no kid left home without knowing how to sew, and so I simply pulled out Francie's sewing machine and got to work designing a lighter pack that would allow me to carry what I needed without overburdening me. What if I made it like a tall duffel bag, with just one big cinchable opening at the top? Did I need the internal frame? How effective were those padded straps in protecting my shoulders anyway? I always came home bruised despite the padding. Was a waist belt a true necessity?

THE PACK, THOUGH, COMPLETELY EMPTY, WEIGHED A WHOPPING SEVEN AND A HALF POUNDS. SEVEN AND A HALF POUNDS OF NOTHING EXCEPT A HOLLOW CONTAINER!

I see now how I'm a little different from other people. I think many folks who read Jardine's book (it was huge among backpackers in the '90s) probably took a few hints from his experience but figured there was only so much they could do to reduce their weight and were simply happy to make an improvement on that front. Not me. I went hog wild, playing with backpack patterns I was developing, trying different fabrics. What about all those zippers? (Zippers weigh a ton.) Were they truly necessary?

Ray Jardine had used a pattern for an Alpine Rucksack for his own pack, and I ordered the pattern. When it arrived, though, I realized it would be way too small for me, so I pretty much made up one of my own. The first one I created was a massively huge pack (I got a little carried away making sure it would be big enough) with no frame whatsoever and purple webbing. I made the shoulder straps hollow so I could shove my sleeping socks in there for padding, thus having the socks fill two purposes. For a waist belt, I used a piece of two-inch-wide webbing. I thought it was pretty great. I filled it up and brought it over to Read to see what he thought.

He admired the design and looked it over before hoisting it onto his shoulders. "It's kind of hard to carry," he said. "I mean, there's a lot of stuff in there and so it feels kind of rough on the back."

I was disappointed. Yes, I'd cut out pretty much all the padding, and what I'd created was fairly primitive, but I thought I was on a roll. Plus, this pack weighed only about a pound. I'd just cut down the overall weight I'd have to carry by six and a half pounds—a huge amount! But if it felt awkward on the back, that wasn't going to be a good long-term solution. Back to the sewing machine.

Of course, I'd eventually have to address the pack's contents as well. Even if my one-pound pack worked, I was still going to be shoving something close to sixty pounds of stuff into it. An improvement, yes, but not enough. As I found ways to whittle down the weight inside the pack, I kept fiddling with the pack itself and designed what I called the G1, using my first initial to identify it. Instead of an internal frame, I designed a pocket into which a backpacker's Z-pad, the accordioned cell-foam sleeping pad many of us used, could fit, offering back support without the added weight of a frame. Soon, the G1 morphed into the G2 and then the G3, every iteration taking advantage of what I'd learned with the previous model.

Over-the-top Austrian yodeling music played on the PA as Ken Hollister, one of the other Scout leaders, and I, both wearing grey old-fashioned sweatsuits, summoned the Scouts around us for *Lightening Up with Hans & Franz*, a takeoff of the *Saturday Night Live* sketch featuring Austrian bodybuilders who don't do much but show off their muscles and claim friendship with Arnold Schwarzenegger. The silly *SNL* skit was something boys in the 1990s loved, and so we vamped as these two clueless guys with thick Austrian accents who demonstrated some of the principles Read and I were discovering about lighter gear.

"Hey Hans," I called to Ken, who played opposite my Franz. "You ready to go backpacking?"

He had prepared himself for this moment with a huge external frame backpack loaded to the gills, a big bear cannister, and all kinds of gear strapped on his back. "I am all set!" he said proudly. He was a big construction guy and puffed out his chest to good effect.

"Good. I'm all ready to go too." I hammed up the accent, shouldering my noticeably smaller, lighter pack. "I got everything I need."

"Impossible!" Ken said, feigning bewilderment. "You can't have everything. Look at that puny pack!" (On *SNL*, the characters were always making fun of skinny guys, so this played right into the moments the boys loved.)

Ken and I, as Hans and Franz, then unpacked our packs to show each other what we had inside.

"I have this tent," he said as he pulled out a massive shelter while I revealed my tiny tarp. He unpacked a bulky sleeping bag while I showed off my lightweight compressible one. By the time we'd finished the skit, the boys had seen that I was able to carry all I needed for a week in the wilderness without having to lug a huge and heavy pack. I cued the yodeling music and the boys started faking their own Austrian accents. My point had been made.

I guess you could say it was around that time that I started proselytizing for lighter gear, and not just among the Boy Scouts. I was so excited by what I'd discovered, I wanted to share the wealth, spreading the gospel of lighter gear. When there was a new dad on a Scout trip with a huge pack, I'd strike up a conversation as we hiked along.

"Nice pack you got there."

The other dad would tell me the pack's brand and that he'd just gotten it at REI.

"Oh, I've heard about those! Would you mind if we traded packs for a bit so I can check it out and see how it feels?" I asked. They usually proudly agreed.

We'd walk alongside each other for a bit, maybe a mile. The other hiker was often quiet during this stretch, realizing with each step he took just how much lighter my pack felt on his back. I'd comment again on how well their pack fit and ask questions about it and why they'd chosen it.

At this point, my targets fell into one of two categories. The smart ones started to ask questions. "What exactly do you have in here?" With that opening, I'd explain the ultralight philosophy and the options I'd chosen as we walked along. It got those hikers thinking. The others, those who were set in their ways and didn't want to have to reconsider their choices, didn't ask questions or engage. They weren't ready for a change, and that was fine. I didn't need to convince anyone, but I was happy to share what I knew with those who were interested.

After a mile, we'd swap packs again and be on our own way. I knew that those who had questioned me would be making changes soon.

By 1998, I was again backpacking with the Scouts, this time to Land's End in the Eastern Sierra, along with Read and Brian and all the other older Scouts. I'd made great strides in reducing my weight, getting rid of the large pack I had initially overengineered. I'd also discarded a lot of the extra clothes I used to bring, weighing each item and choosing the lightest option, slowly winnowing my load.

On this outing, the last one of Brian's Scout career before he would be named an Eagle Scout and graduate high school, I carried my newest iteration, the fledgling G4, while Brian shouldered my previous iteration, the G3. Made out of silnylon, the synthetic fabric of Brian's pack had been created by impregnating thin woven nylon with liquid silicone, making a fabric strong for its weight, the silicone improving the nylon's tear strength. What I hadn't taken into account in that pack's design, though, was that many boys and backpackers in general would not treat the gear I'd developed with the kind of kid gloves it needed.

I STARTED PROSELYTIZING FOR LIGHTER GEAR, AND NOT JUST AMONG THE BOY SCOUTS. I WAS SO EXCITED BY WHAT I'D DISCOVERED, I WANTED TO SHARE THE WEALTH, SPREADING THE GOSPEL OF LIGHTER GEAR.

At the trailhead, Brian set his pack down on a rock like everyone else, and soon a small hole appeared. Day after day, when stopping for lunch to have a little break, or setting up the night's camp, or setting down the pack, he didn't scour the area first to get rid of any stray twigs or feel the surface of the granite rock to make sure it was smooth before dropping his delicate pack. He didn't exactly drag the pack along behind him, but he didn't baby it as I had when I was testing it. As a result, new holes appeared each day.

By the end of our trip, Brian came down the trailhead with a resigned look on his face and the backpack carried on the front of his torso. His hands gripped the pack's bottom, keeping all his gear from escaping from between the shredded fragile fabric that remained at the pack's base. Apparently, in my efforts to get as light as possible with that pack, I'd overshot the mark.

(So as to not waste that pack, I reconditioned it, and it later traveled the California sections of the Pacific Crest Trail, carried by Damian Chouinard, a winemaker from Castro Valley whom I befriended on a hike and invited into our home to stay for a week to both recover from his hiking thus far and to lighten his pack. He was glad to learn ways that would save his suffering body.)

I went back to the drawing board yet again, now fine-tuning the G4 and feeling like I had it down. The pack offered a good balance—enough volume, 4,400 cubic inches, to carry a lot of lightweight stuff. The bottom of the pack pooched out so you didn't need to overcompress your sleeping bag. Three large mesh pockets surrounded the pack so you could store easy-to-reach items at your fingertips. I played with two iterations of this pack. The top of both versions was made of coated ripstop nylon. The bottom portion of the lighter pack utilized 200 denier oxford, while 330 denier Cordura covered the bottom of the heavier one. I'd learned to make sure the bottoms were sturdy! The lighter one came in at twelve ounces, while the heavier one was just over that. Success!

Yes, it had taken at least four iterations, as well as many more minor modifications, but anything worth doing right often involves a series of trials and failures. As an engineer, I knew not to be alarmed when I didn't get it right with my first attempt. Most things can be further refined from their current state.

By this time, I was hiking more with Read Miller than with the Scouts since Brian had graduated and Grant wasn't really into the back-packing scene. Read was doing the PCT in sections, and whenever I could get time off work, I'd join him, putting my gear to the test. I had resumed using bamboo chopsticks as tent stakes, putting them to double duty, and designed lightweight trekking poles that doubled as the tarp poles.

Before each outing, Read and I weighed our packs just as we were closing the trunk of the car to take off. If we weighed them before that moment, we'd be tempted to add an item or two we were sure we couldn't live without—"just in case"—and throw off the scientific vibe we were after. These weigh-ins became our tradition.

We were leaving that Friday morning for the Whitewater Canyon section of the PCT, when we each hung our packs (minus food and water) from a digital fishing scale in Read's driveway. Twelve pounds! We had done it! We had achieved what we'd been after. We erupted into a happy dance of middle-aged men right there in the suburban dawn. We were on our way.

WHEREAS BEFORE I USED A GEAR LIST TO MAKE SURE I DIDN'T LEAVE ANYTHING BEHIND, MY GEAR LIST NOW BECAME A VALUABLE TOOL FOR EXAMINING EVERYTHING I PLANNED TO BRING.

And on the trail that followed, we felt so much better. We could do many more miles. With the Scouts, ten to twelve miles a day had seemed a lot, but now we were covered twenty to twenty-five with the same effort. Since I got only so much time off work, it was important to me to see as much as I could. To reach this point, though, we'd had to increase our outdoors skills, get good at setting up tarps rather than tents and handling the weather with fewer tools, and become more agile in our thinking. It felt good.

My gear list, meanwhile, went through its own conceptual readjustment. Whereas before I used a gear list to make sure I didn't leave anything behind, my gear list now became a valuable tool for examining everything I planned to bring and forcing me ask two crucial questions about each item: (1) Did I really need it? (2) Was there a lighter alternative? By using this process, I'd gotten lean and mean.

Meanwhile, on the pack creation front, I had finished tweaking what I figured was my final iteration, the G4. With that completed, I thought my gear geeking-out days were done.

But on the trail, I'd pass other backpackers, and many wanted to stop and ask about my pack. I would explain to them what I'd done and how I'd created it. Word got around on the various listservs (an early form of social media), like Backpacking Light and PCT-L, composed mostly of hikers doing the PCT. The fact that I had designed a one-pound pack got a lot of attention, and I got inquiries by mail, email, and phone. Could I share my instructions, please?

I wrote up what I had done and created a series of crude diagrams I thought would be easy to follow, with measurements of exactly how to cut the fabric and where to sew it. The whole pack had been designed around my own physique and personal preferences, but soon others were able to adapt it to their own idiosyncrasies. I made my rudimentary pattern available to anyone who asked, once again following the ethos that had been shown to me by others' generosity: to give away to others what had enriched my own life. (How I learned that lesson will be what we cover in the next chapter.)

At the time, I had no idea I would be starting an ultralight backpacking company that would do millions a year in sales. I was just passing along what I'd discovered in the hopes that whoever followed my pattern might also, like me, be able to take less and do more. As you will see, this blossomed into the foundation for many other lessons, and it's the reason I have lived such a blessed life, but it all began by making sure I lightened my load, first with my backpack and then with everything else.

LESSON 4

Be Kind

THIS LESSON MAY SOUND A LITTLE TOO OBVIOUS, BUT WHEN someone is in the middle of a wilderness, simple acts of kindness and generosity can be transformative if not life saving. I have listed it early in the book because I think it is so foundational. When we offer up what we have, both the receiver and the giver are enriched. We are not alone. Not everything rests on our individual shoulders. Recognizing this truth allows us to give up the myth of self-suffi-ciency and opens the way to making do with less. While kindness definitely has a "do more" component, it is only when we take less from life, and create margin, that we are able to help others. And it is only when we focus less on ourselves that we gain the ability to notice those around us and how we might impact their lives in posi-tive ways. That is why kindness and generosity are foundational to embracing a "take less" philosophy.

Still, this was a lesson I had to learn. In other words, being generous and kind was not natural for me at first. But at a young age I was on the receiving end of a generous act that I have never forgotten and has been a model for me ever since.

It was 1976, America's bicentennial year. Red, white, and blue bunting hung from courthouses, libraries, city halls, and schools.

The air was filled with Sousa marches and an excitement to celebrate this nation that had been founded only two hundred years earlier.

I was nearly eighteen and had graduated high school the day before I took off on my bike to see all I could of America—one of the first experiences that formed my "take less, do more" philosophy and set me on the path to developing ultralight backpacking gear.

As my senior year began winding down, I'd started thinking about bicycling across this great land as a way to celebrate not only my release from secondary school but also the country's birthday. I wasn't the only one doing this. Whole groups, often with ten to twelve riders and a group leader, undertook the 4,250-mile route. Those doing the official Bikecentennial crossed ten states, twenty-two national forests, two national parks, and 112 counties between Astoria, Oregon, and Yorktown, Virginia, following a set route that wove through small towns on mostly rural, low-traffic roads.

The organization that launched the Bikecentennial later turned into Adventure Cycling and now offers all kinds of routes. This type of bike-packing has become a well-established adventure travel option now, but back then it was just a crazy idea that ended up having sticking power. In 1976, organizers said 4,100 riders participated in Bikecentennial, but that count didn't include me and my ragtag group. For me, having a "less curated" adventure was my strong preference at the time—still is!—and so I made a plan that didn't follow what all the others were doing and did it my own way.

In high school I'd been very active in the Outing Club. I think I was the president of the club by the end of my time there, and I was heavily involved in the logistics and planning of our trips. We'd done a number of bicycling adventures—up to New Hampshire and Vermont and then down to Cape Cod and back, on the road for a week at a time with a group of about twenty of us. While there certainly must have been adult group leaders along on those treks, they did a good job of staying in the background, because I don't remember them much, or their help. Which was fine. I was good at organizing the group, creating gear lists, and making sure everyone had what would be needed. Those were great trips and gave me an early taste of what was ahead.

Given that experience, I decided to bicycle my way across the entire country and made plans to do so—solo. I wanted a big adventure. I had no other real reason. You remember what it's like to be young and want to do something big? I loved that feeling, and lucky for me, it's been a thread weaving through all of my life. But this was the first time I prepared myself to do a vast exploration completely on my own.

I was giddy with excitement. My mom, who'd been quite an avid adventurer herself, didn't raise undue concerns or stand in the way. It wasn't like I was trying to get out from under her thumb or run away from anything at home. I just wanted to see the larger world and to do so under my own steam.

Three guys I knew from the Outing Club got wind of my plans. Guy Holappa and Todd Sunderland, who had played on the tennis team together, and Mark Howard, who was a year older, asked if they could come too. Sure, why not? The more, the merrier. Together, we made plans and sketched out routes.

At the time, I had hoped to go to college at some point and had notions about becoming a foreign language interpreter. I had enjoyed studying French, Latin, and Greek and could see myself doing that, but I had no set plans for my future. I'd have this big adventure first, and then I'd figure out the rest.

Preparing for this trip was likely when the seeds of what would later become my fascination with designing gear took root. First, I started by sewing some of my own gear, using Frostline Kits, a Colorado-based company that produced sew-it-yourself sets for outdoor gear. I also ordered from Holubar, a mail-order business that sold do-it-yourself kits for sewing down vests and jackets. Meanwhile, I tinkered with my own designs.

Getting ready to cycle forty-two hundred miles, I realized that even on a bike, lighter was better, so I drilled holes in my toothbrush handle to make it lighter and decided I'd use bamboo chopsticks for eating since they were many times lighter than the steel spoon-and-fork options available at that time. My sleeping rig for the summer was a nylon cord hammock and 2.2 oz./sq. yd. urethane-coated ripstop nylon tarp I sewed that could be hung over a nylon rope above the hammock for coverage. To keep bugs off, I sewed a giant tube of netting that had hook and loop on one end, so I could pull it over myself and seal it behind my head. The chopsticks did double duty as tent stakes when needed during the night, then I wiped them off and used them to eat during the day. These days, I travel to Japan periodically to give talks and to hike, and my friends there are often impressed with my chopstick skills. When chopsticks are all you have to eat with, trust me, you get lots of practice.

I HAVE ALWAYS ENJOYED THE CONTEMPLATIVE NATURE OF BICYCLING OR WALKING LONG DISTANCES, THE WAY THE MIND CAN WANDER AND FLIT ABOUT AS THE BODY DOES WHAT YOU'VE INSTRUCTED IT TO DO, WORKING ON A KIND OF AUTOPILOT.

The three other boys and I loaded up our panniers, awaiting the morning after graduation when we'd finally be free to leave. Guy planned to sleep in a hammock like me, while Todd and Mark would share a tent. As these were the pre-internet days, we didn't have a way to properly lay out our route in great detail, but we had a general plan. We charted a cross-country trek in blue highlighter on a map of the whole nation, but as we entered each new state, we planned to stop at the first gas station to get a road map specific to that particular state and then plot our course forward in more detail.

To prepare for this trek, I'd been saving cash. When I was younger, I'd had my own business doing lawn maintenance and snow removal. I supplemented that income with a job at a vitamin store. Now, my panniers held pretty much my entire life savings, about $350 in American Express traveler's checks. I was ready to go.

The night before we took off, I didn't have any great anxiety, just the normal worries: *Am I in shape? Will my bike stay in good working order? Will we find adequate water sources?* I don't remember thinking about the distance we'd eventually cover or worrying much about it, but I guess that's simply the ignorance (some might say boldness) of youth. I had been asked by some folks how I was training for the trip, and I thought that was a silly question. How do you prepare yourself to ride sixty to eighty miles a day, every day, for the next six weeks? By riding sixty to eighty miles a day, and that was pretty much what we planned to do starting on day one. No need to train, just get going.

I didn't know then that I was leaving the East Coast permanently, starting off on my adult life in a way I didn't fully recognize at the time, but I was ready for this big adventure.

We pushed off from Amherst, Massachusetts, with a modest crowd of about thirty friends and family to cheer us on, and after a few miles settled in for what would be a long and memorable haul. I have always enjoyed the contemplative nature of bicycling or walking long distances, the way the mind can wander and flit about as the body does what you've instructed it to do, working on a kind of autopilot. We took the smaller roads, roughly paralleling Route 80, my feet going round and round on the pedals, sweat dripping down my back, appreciating being on the quiet but open road with my pals.

The trip provided my first real epic adventure and gave me a taste for what I would continue to hunger for my entire life: time to be both meditative and active, to see and smell the world around me in an intimate way, and, ultimately, to see where and how I fit in the bigger equation.

Whenever we stopped for food, people would ask us what we were doing. At the beginning of the trip, they'd ask where we'd come from. If we said "Massachusetts," that was just the next state over, so people thought our outing was no big deal. We quickly learned that everything is relative. If we said we'd come from Massachusetts but we were headed to California, then they really perked up. As we got closer to the end of the trip, we had to invert the wording. By then, the fact we were *heading* to California didn't sound like much—it was now maybe one state over—but when we pointed out that we'd *come* from Massachusetts, people appreciated the scope of what we'd accomplished and cheered us on.

One time, we stopped at a gas station early in the morning to get a map. The clerk was so impressed with what we were doing, he roused the chief of police from his bed to come down and also called the local newspaper reporter to take a group picture. A copy of that picture was sent to the folks back home, who then made sure it ran in the local Amherst paper. Alas, we failed to point out that the unidentified guy in the picture with us was the chief of police of that town, and the Amherst paper identified him as a gas station attendant. Oops. They ended up having to run a correction. Still, we felt a little like celebrities.

All in all, it was glorious to be out on our own and figuring our way forward. I think I called my mom maybe twice over those six weeks.

As we made our way through the middle part of the country, it was too hot to cycle efficiently through the middle of the day, so we started riding at night. We lashed flashlights to our bike frames and rode into the wee hours on those rural roads with almost no traffic, pedaling until about two or three in the morning and then finding a place to sleep. We had great luck with finding old rest stops along the roads, places that had since been bypassed by Interstate 80. At those rest stops we could usually find some trees, necessary for me and Guy to string up our hammocks, and a grass patch for the other two to pitch their tent, along with running water and toilets. We had all we needed.

Late one night, we were riding on a completely desolate road and decided to stop and lie down on the rough macadam surface for a brief rest. The pastureland on either side of us was fenced off, so we couldn't make camp there. Since we hadn't seen a car the entire time we'd been riding, we figured the roadway itself would be safe, and if a car came along, we would hear and see it in plenty of time. We all collapsed, grateful to stop moving for a bit. Todd tuned his little transistor radio to a station playing '70s pop tunes—Captain & Tennille and KC and the Sunshine Band. As the music played into the pitch-black night, we were each lost in our own thoughts. I had just closed my eyes when I heard a low rumbling sound. Curious, I clicked on my flashlight. Next to us alongside the fencing, a herd of cattle had come over, curious about these strangers. They stood there looking at us, lowing, having been drawn by the music, keeping watch over us like bovine guardian angels.

Looking back I can see that, as eighteen-year-old boys, our ideas about how to fuel ourselves to ride sixty to eighty miles a day left something to be desired. For breakfast, we'd chow down on Hostess doughnuts or Pop-Tarts—nothing even relatively healthy. At lunchtime, we'd stop in whatever small town we might find ourselves passing through to buy a loaf of cheap white bread, a jar of peanut butter, and a jar of jelly. We'd pass it around and make sandwiches until everything was gone. All my life I'd grown up eating my mom's homemade whole wheat bread, but for this one summer it was a treat to eat the fluffy white Wonder Bread–type bread. That was my one and only white-bread summer.

We had brought a stove with us but seldom used it. For dinners, we got the occasional can of chili or some ramen at a market, but mostly we stopped for fast-food burgers. At Burger Chef, you could get a burger and as much salad as you could eat for 97 cents. Afterward, we'd sometimes buy a half-gallon box of ice cream, then sit cross-legged in a circle in a field and pass the carton between us until it was finished. When you bring chopsticks to a spoon fight, you'd better get good in a hurry if you want your share of ice cream, and I did. Somewhere along the way, we all decided it was time to start chewing tobacco. We were young boys on the cusp of becoming men. What can I say?

In addition to the countless ideas I began to germinate for ways of making gear lighter and more functional, this trip was remarkable for the lessons it taught me about kindness.

We were in Van Tassell, Wyoming, on July 10. I remember the date because the day before had been my eighteenth birthday and we'd gone to a little fast-food stand to get hamburgers and shared a birthday cake. The wife of the guy who owned the fast-food joint had slipped us six bucks when she saw we were celebrating. It was a good time, but by the next morning, the tension that had been on a low simmer between our various personalities reached a boiling point.

For weeks, Todd and Mark had been sharing a tent. Todd snored, and the noise he made kept Mark awake at night. Mark complained all day long about it and never missed an opportunity to torment Todd. Mark was pretty nasty about it, taunting Todd and berating him. Yes, sleeping is important, I get it, but Mark was downright mean in the way he spoke to Todd. Because of this, Todd had taken to sleeping on picnic tables whenever we stayed in rest stops so as to not disturb Mark, making himself smaller and more invisible as time went on. We were all getting a little sick of witnessing Mark mistreat Todd. And for whatever reason—maybe Mark was particularly nasty in his complaints that day—this one particular morning after my birthday, I had had it.

"Todd and I are taking off on our own," I announced without consulting Todd, laying out all our pooled money and splitting it into two. Guy and Mark tried to talk me out of my plan, but I was determined. When someone treats you badly, or treats your friend badly, it never ends well and seldom improves. The only way for us to have peace was to get away from the source of the strain.

Todd looked bewildered. The last thing he wanted was to be the source of more tension. I told him to follow me. "You've taken enough," I said.

I knew somehow that kindness was an important component in life satisfaction, and the fact that Mark was mistreating Todd outraged my sense of fair play. Still, while I easily spotted unkindness in others, I was not so adept at spotting it in myself. To this point, I'd been pretty hard core about making the miles I thought we needed to, driving us all to achieve my ambitions. We didn't need to be anywhere by a set date, yet I pushed us all forward as though we were under a deadline. Sixty to eighty miles a day, minimum, I demanded. I guess I became a bit overbearing.

I can see the dynamic clearly now, though I was pretty oblivious to it at the time. Still, when I think of all the wonderful times of fun and fellowship I have had on group trips since then, I can see what my unkindness cost us. As I was driving the group to keep up with my ambitions, Mark and Guy (and maybe even Todd too) would have been happier to go at a slower pace and really see the towns we were passing through, to take in the scenery—something I've come to appreciate. To tell you the truth, this concept of "taking my time" is something I still struggle with. I know there's lots to be seen and experienced by going slower and really being present, but my desire to achieve certain outcomes sometimes interferes with my ability to witness and participate in what's unfolding in the moment. I'm making progress, though.

Either way, I convinced Todd that he and I were ready to move at a quicker clip, and that was another reason to leave the others. At the time, I couldn't see that elements of unkindness were on both sides.

Still, whatever precipitated it, the group splitting apart seemed the wisest course, and we did so with as few hard feelings as possible. For the next few days, Todd and I kept running into Guy and Mark in the various towns we stopped in along on the way. Eventually they fell behind our quicker pace, but we all completed the journey safely and made it home.

Before we split up, the most memorable day of the trip had occurred in rural Chatsworth, Illinois, in the southeast portion of the state, population about a thousand. Keep in mind, on this journey we slept wherever we could. We had no money for hotels or campgrounds, so we usually found a spot by the side of the road if there wasn't a rest stop nearby. Our favorite strategy in the more rural parts of the country was to stop as we rode through a small town, go and knock on someone's front door, explain what we were doing, and ask if it was okay if we slept on their front lawn for the night. I don't remember anyone ever turning us down.

Once or twice we slept in city parks. One time, we'd ridden late into the night and slept the morning away in the shade of a huge elm in a public park. I awoke to hear a mom scolding her small child. "Get away from that man!" We looked (and smelled) homeless and scary to her. I can't say I blame her; I might have reached the same conclusion. Another time, in Nevada, we ended the day in a fairly good-size city. We arrived too late to see if someone would let us sleep on their lawn, so we loitered at the city park until darkness fell, then scattered and stretched out our sleeping bags on the expanse of grass. Around 2:00 a.m. I was awakened by a strange noise that inserted itself into my dreams. It was a rhythmic ka-SWOOSH, ka-SWOOSH.

My sleep-addled brain struggled to make sense of the noise, until I heard a torrent of drops falling nearby. I panicked, realizing the park's giant Rain Bird sprinklers had come on. Inch-worming my way out of my sleeping bag as quickly as I could, I could see Todd doing likewise. Once freed from our sleeping bags, we ran in all different directions, grabbing our gear and trying to evade the sprinkler blasts that seemed to be arcing out of the moonless sky from every conceivable point of the compass. Needless to say, we didn't get any more sleep that night.

But in rural Illinois, we had an encounter that has stayed with me vividly all these years. Following our usual plan, the other three guys waited by the bikes in the street as I went up to the door of the modest house and knocked. An elderly man answered. I was eighteen, so who knows how old he actually was—maybe younger than I am now—but he seemed old to me at the time.

"Of course you can stay here," he said, after I explained our request. "I think you'll find it more comfortable on the side of the house, though, rather than the front yard."

I thanked him. As we were setting up camp, he came over to chat with us about our trip so far. I think he was living vicariously through our exploits. "What time will you be leaving in the morning?" he asked.

"We try to cover a lot of miles," I explained. "So we usually hit the road by seven."

He looked crestfallen. I paused to see what the problem was.

"It's just . . . my wife," he explained. "She'd love to make you a proper breakfast. Both of us would. But she has really bad arthritis. The mornings are particularly difficult for her." If we could hang around until later in the day and her arthritis warmed up a bit, he said, they would happily serve us a proper breakfast.

But I hated the thought of losing time and progress. My need to make tracks—where exactly did I think I needed to get to?—impelled me to speak on behalf of the group and decline his offer, without checking whether the group agreed with me. "That's okay," I said. "It's very kind of you both, but we don't expect breakfast. We usually just eat something cold and then head out. Still, we appreciate your hospitality."

As we were settling down for the night, watching fireflies light up the dusk that was now turning to full-on night, he came out again.

"We really would love to make you breakfast," he said and proffered a box of Hostess powdered mini donuts. "You could use something more substantial than this, but I'm afraid it's the best we can do."

"Thank you, so much. You've already been far too kind."

When he went back into their house, the lights winked off for the night.

The next morning, in the early dawn hours, the air was fresh and a little humid as we packed up. The town was still drowsing, and we would be on our way in minutes. But then the door to the house opened and the man came across the dew-soaked lawn.

"Follow me," he said, beckoning the four of us. We stopped our packing to trail him into the small clapboard house. The minute we walked in, we could smell the goodness. Bacon and sausage. Pancakes. Their modest table was laden with a spread of food, the likes of which I'd never seen. Fried eggs, homestyle potatoes, handmade biscuits, gravy, juice. This older couple, likely far from wealthy, had fought through morning arthritic stiffness and the early hour to make us a feast. They endured pain and inconvenience because I had insisted on leaving early. They must have used up their own breakfast groceries for the entire coming week, so profligate were they with their big-heartedness. I wondered later if they went hungry over the coming mornings due to their generosity.

But did we ever appreciate it! We'd gone weeks without a hot breakfast, and this was so lavish. If I had not been so bent on making miles, perhaps this delightful offering could have been given with a little more ease. Either way, though, we ate every bite, syrup and sausage grease glistening our lips, while the couple looked on with faces awash in joy at our delight.

To this day, more than forty-five years later, it brings tears to my eyes thinking of how much pain the wife endured to cook up that huge spread for hungry strangers. In the six weeks of traveling across country, this act of kindness and generosity is what I recall most often. I have been telling that story for four and a half decades now, and I like to think that for years afterward, that couple told the same story but from their perspective—a tale of four hungry boys on bicycles they served that summer morning in 1976, the way they helped those boys make their dream of cycling to California come true. In this instance, as in all instances of genuine generosity, both the givers and receivers were amply rewarded.

That experience not only taught me about kindness but also reinforced another important lesson. I realized that being connected to others, that being humble, sometimes means not just giving but also being willing to receive. If I always insist on being the giver in every situation, then I'm trying to be in control and to feed my own ego. Plus, the circular nature of giving and receiving stops if I refuse to also receive—which I did in that situation, even as the older man and his wife found a way around my obstinacy.

We need to keep the flow going, to allow the tide of giving and receiving to move both ways. Every person on this planet has talents and unique ways of helping others, and it's wrong to withhold those gifts. Whatever you have to share, do so with open arms. But it's equally wrong to refuse the goodness another offers. Doing so robs a fellow human of their God-given need to be of service to others, to feel that their contribution matters. The couple taught us all that predawn morning that they had something special to add to the world, and they were going to add their gift despite my intransigence, thank goodness. And because they did just that, one morning more than forty-five years ago, a day of decency and kindness, of giving and receiving, resonates in my life to this day.

Take Less, Give More

THE FINAL SCENE FROM THE RIVETING SPIELBERG MOVIE *Schindler's List* plays in my mind over and over again. The film was released over thirty years ago, and when I first saw it, I was reduced to tears. I still can't watch it without being deeply moved.

The movie focuses on Oskar Schindler, a German industrialist, humanitarian, and member of the Nazi Party who was credited with saving the lives of twelve hundred Jews during the Holocaust by employing them in his enamelware and munitions factories in occupied Poland as well as in Bohemia and Moravia.

But in life, as in the film, Schindler didn't start off as a do-gooder.

Initially, he was interested only in the money-making potential of his business, and he hired Jews simply because they were cheaper than Poles, with wages set by the occupying Nazi regime. Later, though, as he came to see that his efforts to help might actually matter, he began shielding his workers without regard to cost. The actions he took had a positive influence on the world, and that feeling that he could make a difference came to mean more to him than money.

As the film progresses, Schindler, in order to keep up appearances as a manufacturing magnate, socialized with Nazi officers, pretending that his motivations for protecting his workers were purely financial. He banned guards from the factory floor in Czechoslovakia, arguing that harsh treatment and executions were detrimental to productivity.

He also rescued children from Auschwitz, claiming that the children's small fingers were necessary for polishing the insides of shell casings.

In reality, Schindler's humanitarian undertaking eventually cost him everything he had. By the war's end, Schindler had spent most of his personal wealth on constructing his camp, providing food for his Jewish workers, and bribing Nazi officials.

Once Germany surrendered to the Allied forces, Schindler, who was still a member of the Nazi Party, was forced to flee his factory. Before he left, his workers presented him with a letter explaining what he had done, signed by every worker at his factory. They also gave him a golden ring with a Talmudic inscription: "Whoever saves one life saves the world entire."

Moved by the workers' gratitude, Schindler broke down crying, lamenting to his assistant, Itzhak Stern, that he might have saved more people if he had been willing to let go of more of his most valuable possessions.

"I could have got more out. I could have got more. I don't know. If I'd just... I could have got more." He looked at his car. "Why did I keep the car? Ten people right there. Ten more people." He removed his Nazi pin from his lapel. "This pin. Two people. This is gold. Two more people. He would have given me two for it, or at least one. One more person. A person, Stern. For this." He sobbed.

That is the part that haunts me.

Few of us, we think, will ever be in a position to help people the way Schindler did. Our lives are so much smaller, we possess so little power, we have too few opportunities to shape the world for the better. But is that actually true? If the saying on the golden ring presented to Schindler is accurate—"Whoever saves one life saves the world entire"—then perhaps our efforts to ease the sufferings of those around us, even one person, are much more profound and valuable than we realize.

I understand it's ridiculous to put suffering on the level of the Holocaust on par with anything any of us might do, but what I want you to realize is that *every* effort you make to help someone else has a weighty impact. Perhaps shoveling your neighbor's driveway, or anonymously paying for a child's flute lesson, or bringing soup to someone who is sick is not going to change the course of history. But you never know. It might alter in some tiny yet important way the course of that person's individual trajectory. As others have said, "I've learned that people will forget what you said, people will forget what you did, but people will never forget how you made them feel." Sometimes, helping someone to feel safe, protected, seen, or heard has a profound effect.

Early on I adopted a concept elucidated by the author Antoine de Saint-Exupéry: "[It seems that] perfection is attained not when there is nothing more to add, but when there is nothing more to remove."[1] Over the years, as I worked on civil engineering puzzles and tinkered in my free time with developing lightweight backpacking gear, this concept guided me. It also touched on so much in life by asking me to focus on finding what is essential.

And yet, while Saint-Exupéry speaks of "perfection," I have come to realize that maybe not everything *can* be perfected. Maybe making progress as a human, developing a spiritual framework, and engaging with others and my own work in a way that creates good-will is actually more important than achieving perfection.

Still, his words guide me, getting me to that place where nothing else can be taken away. This is the kernel of ultralight backpacking, but it's also a crucial way to look at life.

But how do we position ourselves to give to others from our time, our resources, our talents if we need everything we have just to make it through the day? This is where the idea of taking less comes into play. Minimalism. Learning to get by with only what we truly require.

I think of it in terms of backpacking. When I carry only what I need, I have a greater capacity than I'm using at that moment; I have not maxed myself out. Yes, that means I can log more miles and see more of this spectacular world if that's what's on the docket, but it also means I have the ability to help someone else who is struggling.

I was recently hiking in Buckskin Gulch in southern Utah with a group of people including my lovely wife, Francie. It became apparent that, due to her hip problems, the weight of her backpack was taking a toll on her body. I could see it in her stride, the way she was slowing down, the hidden grimaces that maybe only a spouse would notice. She was doing this trip to please me and to be with some of our mutual friends, but backpacking isn't really her thing, and it was now costing her plenty.

The fact that I was carrying a pack of not much more than ten pounds in weight, including food and water, meant that I was in a position to help. I could sling my pack on my front and carry her pack on my back, allowing her hips the break they desperately needed.

How many ways in life are we able to help carry someone else's burden, figuratively and literally? They are countless if we look for them. And I would venture that, like Oskar Schindler, when we put ourselves out in this way, we find that the emotional riches we receive are much more valuable than whatever it is we think we may have given up.

Minimalism is about a lifestyle of intentionally owning less. It's not about carrying or owning the *fewest* number of things possible but rather owning just the right amount of things so we can focus on the priorities we've set for our lives. How much is just right? With minimalism, I embrace those things I most value, and I consciously remove anything that distracts me from my rich and abundant life. This principle applies to many areas of life besides possessions. I've heard it said that the richest person is not the one who owns the most but the one who needs the least.

I appreciate that sentiment, and minimalism has taught me to embrace that form of richness.

THIS IS WHERE THE IDEA OF TAKING LESS COMES INTO PLAY. MINIMALISM. LEARNING TO GET BY WITH ONLY WHAT WE TRULY REQUIRE.

What this means in practice impacts many parts of my life. For example, I don't look for the cheapest item when shopping; I try to purchase what is high quality and will last, and I tend to spend money on experiences rather than things. To that end, I eschew activities that pull me away from fully living my life, like social media or overscheduling my days. When I'm too distracted or busy, I miss out on opportunities to really appreciate my life and to be of service.

I *do* try to schedule my life in a way that makes me as healthy as possible, like exercising regularly and eating a wholesome diet. Habits shape our lives, both daily and over a lifetime. By removing habits that obstruct my fullness of life, I feel better and more focused on what matters to me. For instance, because I care about both the health of my body and the health of this planet, I tend to choose a plant-based diet. That said, if invited to dinner at someone's house or if circumstances are such that following that diet is not easy or possible, I remain flexible and eat whatever is offered.

The principles of minimalism also come into play in my speech. I think about the words of Bernard Meltzer, a radio host who ran an advice call-in show from 1967 to the 1990s. If I remember, it goes something like this:"Before you speak, ask yourself if what you are going to say is true, is kind, is necessary, is helpful. If the answer is no, maybe what you are about to say should be left unsaid."

As part of this effort, I strive to avoid negative self-talk as much as possible. We are often our toughest critic, allowing emotions like blame, regret, and fear to shape how we see things. Just changing how we speak to ourselves about what's happening and choosing our thoughts intentionally—taking custody of our thoughts—can free up our mental capacity to see things more objectively.

And though many self-help gurus will tell you to set and go for your biggest, wildest goals, my thoughts on that subject are a little different. I regularly try to reduce the number of goals I'm striving to achieve so that I can focus as clearly as possible on each and am not splitting my attention and efforts. What matters to you? Put that first. Write it down and put it on your bathroom mirror, on your fridge, on your steering wheel. Are the choices you are making today supporting the life you truly desire?

All of this boils down to my own definition of success. The world tells us what success looks like: the big house, the fancy clothes, the sports car, the heaped-on adulation. But I have found the opposite to be true. When I know what matters most to me and I orient my life around those priorities, I experience a kind of peace and calmness that all the money in the world, all the vacation houses, and all the admiration of others cannot buy. No matter how I look at it, my goals remain consistent: to embrace those elements of my life that feed my greatest wishes and passions and to reduce anything that is a distraction from them.

These lessons, as first experienced in the backcountry and then slowly adopted into my personal life, have changed so much, including how Francie and I view money and the resources available to us.

We have both worked hard our entire professional lives and have tried to be good stewards of what we've received. We also made a conscious choice to live below our means in order to be sure we had a margin for error. This came in handy when my own engineering firm was on the rocks after the economy tanked in 1992. Because we'd kept our overhead low, Francie went back to work, and we had the cushion needed to ensure that I could keep the business going without taking a salary for a year while I helped my employees find new jobs. I had asked them to come work with me, and I felt a responsibility to make sure they landed as well as possible in that recessionary climate. When the day finally came for me to shutter that business, I could do so without a sense of failure; I had done all I could to promote it and to care for the people who'd come to work with me, and though eventually the business became untenable, my relationships with those people and with my clients were strong and enriching. That's success in my book.

Francie and I also took this philosophy into our charitable giving. That term, *charitable giving*, sounds so pompous and self-important, and I want to be clear that I don't mean it in that way. What I want to say is that, as fellow humans on this planet, we have a moral responsibility for each other and that, to meet that responsibility, Francie and I developed a way of living up to that obligation that works well for us.

Way back, early in our respective careers, Francie and I decided to set up a separate checking account with its own debit card specifically for the purpose of helping others in need. Every payday, a set percentage of our income went into that account. Initially, we deposited 5 percent. I thought of it (and still do) as our gratitude account, though you could also call it your peace fund, or giving account, whatever works for you.

This money is distinct from a rainy day fund, savings for retirement, or college savings. It is money that we become essentially trustees for, but it is not in our budget. This way, when needs present themselves, we can address those needs independent of whether we happen to be feeling rich or poor in the moment. Because we have this margin, we have been able to bless many people in need over the years. We have supported ministries and organizations monthly that are important to us, but we also maintain a healthy balance with more nontraditional charity. We've been able to write checks on the spot when a need occurs, like to help a person afford a funeral for their son who died in prison. A longtime friend was dying of cancer with no family, and we were there. Another person, also dying of cancer, had a bucket list of travel he wanted to tick off and no financial resources to do so. That's where this kind of account comes into play. We can write a $100 check or one for $10,000 on the spur of the moment if needed. It makes no difference to our monthly budget, because it's already been set aside. It's no longer our money; we're just stewards of it. We've been able to help replace salaries lost due to the coronavirus for people who didn't have other options. By living on less, we've been able to give more.

I PREFER TO LOOK AT THE ONE PERSON I CAN CONTROL—ME—AND ASK IF I AM DOING ENOUGH. AM I COMFORTABLE WITH WHAT I AM DOING TO MAKE A DIFFERENCE?

Even before we decided to set up our separate checking account, I had figured out that when I felt poor, giving to others made me feel rich. When my fledgling engineering company, Pacific Rim Engineering, was based in San Marcos, California, there was a flower shop standing by itself where Mission Avenue crossed the railroad tracks, not far from our office on Rancho Santa Fe Road. It was called the Little Yellow House. One day I came up with a plan and explained it to the owner: I would leave her my credit card info, and when someone came into her shop that looked like they needed a little help, she could use that card and let me know the amount afterward. The stories I got from the shop owner were well worth the sums involved. One day she told me that a young woman had come in to get flowers for a friend who had just found out they had cancer and did not have long to live. The woman appeared to be of very modest means, understandably distraught by the news of her friend. The shop owner showed her small arrangements but noticed the woman couldn't help glancing back continually at a much larger arrangement. Finally, the shop owner told the woman she could have the larger arrangement for the price of the much smaller one, explaining that an anonymous donor was making up the difference. The shop owner didn't even charge the entire difference to my card because she wanted to participate by discounting the arrangement. Generosity often begets more generosity.

Oddly enough, the ability to give away has boomeranged with its own abundance. Though we started with a small percentage, that amount has grown gradually as our income has increased. Some people seem to think that charitable giving should be handled by the ultra-rich, and they always demand to know what the rich are doing with their millions. I prefer to look at the one person I can control—me—and ask if I am doing enough. Am I comfortable with what I am doing to make a difference, without worrying about whether other people are doing what they should?

This may not be true for everyone, but our rule is that if we begin to feel too comfortable with the amount we are giving, we increase the percentage. This has taken us, over the years, from 5 percent of our after-tax income to, now, a significant portion of our pretax income. Everyone is different, but for us, if we don't notice any discomfort caused by our sacrifice, we could probably be giving more. Don't get me wrong; we have plenty. But it's a mindset, a deliberate choice we are making, that creates more margin to help others.

The reality is, though, that when we give to others, we are enriching everyone. We never know when we might be the ones in need, and we have to remain open to accepting help if we find ourselves in difficult straits.

It's interesting to note that after all Oskar Schindler did to save people, he ended up living in Argentina, where he tried raising chickens and then nutria, a small animal valued for its fur. When that business went bankrupt in 1958, he left his wife and returned to Germany, where he had a series of unsuccessful business ventures before declaring bankruptcy in 1963. He suffered a heart attack the next year, which led to a monthlong stay in the hospital. Throughout his misfortunes, though, he remained in contact with many of the Jews he had met during the war, including Itzhak Stern. Schindler, the man who had saved so many, eventually survived on donations sent by *Schindlerjuden* (literally translated from German as "Schindler Jews") from all over the world, reminding me again that giving and receiving are two sides of the same coin.

Balance *Less* with *Enough*

I KEPT TELLING MYSELF I WOULD STOP WHEN I FOUND THE RIGHT place. First, I wanted to get to the top of that next hill, just over there. But as I reached the top, I could see that there was another, higher peak ahead. I should hold off until I made that next summit. Meanwhile, every step was coming at a higher and higher cost. I was thirsty. My legs hurt, and exhaustion seemed to settle like a bag of wet cement around my shoulders.

The quiet was pervasive. Earlier on this expedition, I'd been able to hear a trickle from a stream, a welcome aspect in this stretch of arid desert, along with the paper-bag rustle of wind in the cotton-woods. But now, all water was far behind me. Chaparral and low scrub blanketed the terrain, and an eerie quiet filled the air, broken only by the caw of a crow.

Still, I kept taking steps and telling myself that I could do this. But when I finally crested the peak and reached the place where I'd promised myself I would at last rest and slake my thirst, I still didn't stop. I decided I really should look for shade. It was in the '90s on this desert portion of the Pacific Crest Trail between Tehachapi and Agua Dulce in Southern California, and the heat was taking it out of me. I wasn't feeling well and knew that shade was important, so I kept trudging forward, hoping to find some respite from the sun.

Earlier, I'd been able to notice the beauty of the region and had spent time staring up at the cotton-white clouds suspended, not moving, looking like they had no plans to change shape or be on their way anytime soon. The chaparral, Joshua trees, and layered geology of the terrain were stunning, though most notable had been the deep and abiding solitude. But that had been back when I was still observing things. Now, I'd become like a machine that kept moving forward simply because that's what it had been programmed to do. One foot in front of the other. *There you go. You're getting there.*

I was on one of the most treacherous portions of the PCT, challenging not because of steep cliffs, dangerous mammals, or difficult stream crossings but because of the extreme heat and lack of water. Still, I took that risk with a grain of salt. After all, I was a seasoned backpacker. I knew what I was doing.

I kept pounding on, and when at last I found some welcome shade, believe it or not, I still didn't allow myself to stop. I decided I should wait for the perfect spot, one with not only shade but also a view. That would be even better. I knew I needed to drink water, but it was going to be such a hassle to get to it, so why stop? I kept moving.

In my zeal to do this trip carrying as little weight as possible while also equipping myself with enough water for this extremely arid portion of the trek, I'd come up with what I thought was a handy invention. I'd sewn a fabric tube into which I fit a long water bladder and then wore that around my waist like a belt, which meant I was carrying less weight on my back. Genius! And then, because I was obsessed with keeping the weight I was carrying to an absolute minimum, I'd decided against taking a drinking tube to connect to that bladder. In my book, the tube's weight was excessive for the benefit it provided, so I ditched it. So now, in order to provide myself with water, I had to stop, undo my makeshift water belt, extract the water bladder, unscrew the lid and drink, and then reverse the process to start hiking again. But since the water was nestled right against my core, it had grown warm and not particularly appetizing. Why bother? I kept hiking.

I was backpacking alone, trudging forward, not finding the ideal spot, and slowly realizing I wasn't in good shape. Finally, I had no choice. Or rather, my body made the choice for me. I pulled off the trail when doing so became a sudden biological imperative. Something was clearly wrong.

Despite the sweat-inducing temperatures in this desert land, with the sun focused on me as if through a magnifying glass, I was shivering. I couldn't get warm. I pulled out my sleeping bag and crawled into it, glorying in the heat it provided, thankful that at least I'd changed my mind about bringing the sleeping bag. (I had thought I'd be fine without it.) Now, I drank as much tepid water from my water bladder as I could stomach and promptly fell asleep in the middle of the day.

When I woke, I realized what had happened. This was the second time in my hiking career I'd suffered from heat exhaustion, and I knew the symptoms. I needed to be very careful with myself if I didn't want to become a statistic. Yes, this was one of the more hazardous stretches of the PCT, but the truth was, *I* was to blame for my condition, not the weather or the terrain.

As I lay in the sleeping bag still shivering, but less so now, I thought about my family. Francie would kill me if I died out here. Plus, Brian and Grant, our sons, would be so mad that I'd been careless. I didn't think I was in such bad shape that I might die, but I could've been wrong. I hoped I still had many years left. Still, if it *was* my time to go, maybe I'd get to see our middle son, Derek, in heaven. He'd died before his twentieth birthday after a tough life, having been born with a severe handicap that prevented him from growing and maturing in a healthy way.

Though I mostly thought I was going to be okay, I couldn't help but be annoyed at myself with the thought that I might not be. What a silly reason to die! This trip had begun as an experiment to see just how light a pack I could possibly take, but now I saw I had taken the ultralight idea a smidge too far. My buddy Read and I had been working to see if we could get our base pack weight (not counting food and water) down to under two pounds for this trip. Since we'd be in the desert, we wouldn't need rain gear or tents. We planned to hike at night and sleep during the day; therefore, we'd initially decided to jettison the sleeping bags and warm clothes. (Thank goodness I'd reversed course on the sleeping bag.) No cooking meant we didn't need a stove, pots, or utensils. We were all set to go when Read had a last-minute scheduling conflict. Since I had already taken the time off work, I'd decided to do the trip solo.

I ENJOY MY OPEN-ARMED EMBRACE OF THE WILDERNESS, EXPLORING THE MAGNIFICENCE AND WISDOM OF NATURE, TESTING MY SKILLS AND ABILITIES IN DIFFERENT WAYS, AND EXPERIENCING A SIMPLER EXISTENCE.

Because I would now be traveling alone, I relaxed the guidelines a bit and managed to get my base weight down to just under three pounds (2.89 to be exact), including that very welcome sleeping bag that was now blessedly helping me restore my homeostasis.

Eventually, my thinking grew clearer and I saw the tragic flaw in my water-carrying system. Because my water was so hard to reach and generally unappealing, I had procrastinated in stopping to drink, playing games with myself about wanting the perfect spot. Not finding that ideal location, I'd continued on, repeating this process until I had put myself in a precarious position. I had taken my own penchant for perfectionism, coupled with minimalist hiking, too far, exceeding extreme ultralight (XUL) into what the adventure guide Andrew Skurka calls "Stupidlight."

Thank goodness I survived my mistake with no real harm. But on this trip, I recognized that, like everything in life, there's a tipping point, a place beyond which we've gone too far. Not only in what we put in our backpacks but in how we balance our lives. There are times when we tip over into habits and conditions that don't serve us, not only as outdoors people but as humans. And if we can recognize those tipping points, we can make different choices.

Sure, there are benefits to be gained from minimalism in all parts of our lives, looking for ways to "take less" and "do more." I'd spent a large portion of my life applying these concepts to backpacking. I'd also found the philosophy applied to other areas of my life—be they business related, or dealing with difficulties at home, or simply navigating life in the twenty-first century. My outdoor experiences were simply a metaphor, providing an opportunity to look at all aspects of my life and the choices I made through a new lens. As a result, maybe I would make different choices in the future—like no more waist-hugging water systems, for one. Yes, lightening my load or the loads of others, reducing the weight of the things I carried, both physical and metaphysical, was a great goal, freeing me up to do so much more, but I needed to find the right balance.

When I take off into the wilderness, I leave behind certain elements of my day-to-day life while I embrace new elements. I leave behind the busyness of modern living with its insect-like annoyances of work emails to be addressed, phone calls to be returned, news and social media to be monitored. I also leave obligations I generally enjoy—coffee or lunch with friends, social engagements, creative engineering problems to solve—as well as elements I simply take for granted: my soft bed, flushing toilets, hot showers, potable water at any temperature I select, home-roasted coffee, and my homemade sourdough bread coming out of the oven and smelling of promise and possibility.

While turning my back on those elements of my daily existence, pleasurable and otherwise, I also reach toward a new set of experiences, likewise a combination of pleasurable and otherwise. I enjoy my open-armed embrace of the wilderness, exploring the magnificence and wisdom of nature, testing my skills and abilities in different ways, and experiencing a simpler existence. In the five pounds of gear I typically carry, I have everything I need to be comfortable and safe. The only decisions I generally need to make are when I stop, where I sleep, what food I eat and when, and how much water I will need to get to the next source. With my decision-making reduced to those essentials, I have a lot of space and freedom for my mind to wander—and to wonder.

But in order to leave behind the old and embrace the new in the most satisfying way possible, I have needed to make careful planning decisions, particularly about what I choose to carry. It has taken years of trial and error to know exactly what "my essentials" actually are, and everyone, I've come to understand, has a slightly different list.

In some ways, I've come to see that task—determining for ourselves what's truly essential for our well-being—as one of the most important jobs we can undertake, whether we're talking about backpacking or any other endeavor in life. When we know exactly what we need and how to provide it for ourselves, then we also come to recognize what is *not* essential. Plenty of things and experiences, sometimes even those we've ardently pined for, turn into drains on our precious life energy. They don't add to a blissful existence in the way we'd envisioned they would but rather end up robbing us of enjoyment, just like carrying a too-heavy pack can turn an otherwise delightful outing into a torturous slog. We all know what it's like to have too little, just as I learned when suffering from heat exhaustion in the California desert. But having too much—not just what we carry when we backpack but in every aspect of our lives— can also throw off our balance and make what might be an enjoyable existence into something that must simply be endured. The trick, I have found, is to find our own true balance.

If I hike with a fairly light load on my back containing only those things I genuinely need, I am not constantly thinking about how much work this hike is, how my body hurts, and wondering when it will finally be over. Rather, I am able to enjoy my surroundings and notice the small details—the whorl of a tree stump, the smell of lavender, the specific orange of a monarch butterfly— details I would otherwise be too preoccupied to allow entry into my consciousness.

Similarly, when my life is simplified at home, I have more bandwidth to engage with my surroundings and my neighbors. By embracing thoughtful minimalism and creating margin in my life, I have more space to embrace that which matters most to me. But I only got there by consciously weighing up (get it?) what matters. I ask myself regularly, *What gives me the most joy, and where can I offer my excess to others?* These questions require deep thought and meditation. Instead of simply tallying the weight of the gear in my backpack, this philosophy also asks me to itemize distractions from a thoughtfully lived life, including the obvious ones of money and possessions but also the less evident ones, like fame, the single-minded pursuit of happiness, and the role of technology. (For a good start on this journey, I recommend Joshua Becker's excellent book *Things That Matter*.)

Living in a rich country, there is so much I take for granted: my nice house, a basically unlimited supply of desirable food, clean water, a hot shower, my soft bed, my reliable cars, a wide variety of clothing, easy access to tools and materials, books, the internet . . . the list goes on.

But usually, I don't stop to think about how rich and comfortable I am; I just accept the ease and softness that surround me. That's one of the big benefits of backpacking. Walking, sleeping, cooking, and eating on the ground allows me to wonder anew at the incredible magic of a hot shower. Sleeping for a week on a ⅜" foam torso pad gives me a new appreciation for the box springs, mattress, and memory foam of my California King at home. Thanks to a week-long experience of extreme minimalism, I come back able to more fully appreciate all the richness that makes up my daily life.

Because, let's be honest, it's easy for most of us to see what is lacking, the empty half of the glass. This is especially true at this time in the United States. Social media, television, and movies, even the ads as we browse the internet, constantly remind us of what we *don't* have, suggesting that (1) everyone else *does* have this thing we lack and/or (2) our lives would be so much better if we *did* have it.

Learning to be content has become countercultural. In our environment, we are encouraged to compare ourselves to others who have more and to wonder why we have less. Why not us? To be fair, our system has created a standard of living that is the envy of the world and has lifted millions of people out of poverty. Like many strengths, though, having more and more possessions can become a weakness. When the striving for a better life becomes a constant comparison with those who have more, it engenders some nasty side effects, such as the idea that if we don't have more and consume more, we become bitter and resentful instead of thankful and open. Yet how do we know when we have enough?

As dangerous as this kind of comparison can be, it can also be a powerful tool in fostering gratitude. Nothing helps me realize how blessed I am quite as much as focusing on people who have less. I watched an episode of *30 Days*, Morgan Spurlock's show that asked ordinary Americans to step out of their comfort zone and live in someone else's shoes for thirty days. They profiled an American guy in the Midwest who'd lost his job when the work he did was outsourced to India. He was understandably upset and believed the people in India had "stolen" his job. The TV show then took him to India, where he met the workers who'd been hired to do his job. He went to their homes and saw how simply they lived. By the end of the program, he said he was glad they had "his" job. They had so little and were feeding so many people with "his" job. As a result of that trip and his newly expanded understanding, his attitude completely changed. After meeting those with so much less, he had an entirely different perception of his life, and he knew he would find another job and could acquire different skills.

"These billionaires are so ridiculous," said Makayla, a coworker at Sparrow. A group of us had gone to a local brewery after our shift, sharing beers and deep conversation.

We were discussing generosity and its role in life when Makayla went off on all the ways people like Jeff Bezos were messing up the world by hoarding wealth.

"We don't celebrate when people hoard newspapers and canned goods and Beanie Babies in their houses, do we? That's seen as a kind of mental illness," she said. "There's even a TV show about how harmful hoarding is, limiting a person's ability to move around their own home and often circumscribing their happiness. And yet, in our culture, we celebrate those who hoard ridiculous amounts of money. It's crazy."

Of course, she made some good points, but I brought up another aspect.

"What about those people who are refugees living in a camp in Sudan?" I asked. "They left their entire existence behind, everything they'd ever known, and have had to go forward with only the few things they can carry. Have you ever stopped to think about the fact that, to those people, *you* are Jeff Bezos? Look at all you have. Compared to them, you're hoarding wealth."

We all sat with that for a moment. I wasn't trying to put Makayla on the spot. If anything, I was calling out my own overly blessed life.

I remembered hearing the story of a person sitting on a bus bench with a Nobel Prize–winning scientist on one side and a homeless person on the other. The person in the middle lamented how he'd been so close to ending up like the Nobel Prize winner. If only he'd had a few luckier breaks, such as parents who recognized his talents early on, the best education money could buy, and the opportunity to show his true intellect. We've all felt this way. If only I'd had the right breaks, what I could have done. But how often do we think about the homeless man on the other side? Compared to his experience, perhaps, we've had nothing but good breaks, parents who weren't drug-dependent, say, or simply a stable home life. Or brain chemistry that works the way it's intended and doesn't short out when we need it most. Or the physical ability to hold a job and earn a living. We always look at what we don't have and seldom stop to inventory all the ways our lives have been touched by good fortune and grace.

The brewery conversation got around to a well-known 2010 study by Princeton researchers who found that people tend to feel happier the more money they make, up until a point—which at that time was estimated to be about $75,000 a year per person. After that, happiness levels off. People's well-being, or how they felt about their lives, didn't change. Once you can meet your basic needs, such as access to health care and a safe home environment, you have all the ingredients needed for happiness.[2] Another researcher, Sonja Lyubomirsky, found that people making $30,000 thought they'd need to increase their annual salary to $50,000 to be happy. But those earning $100,000 per year estimated a yearly salary of $250,000 would make them happy.[3] In short, people always think they need a little more money to be happy.

"It's all about equality," Mark added. "The more economic equality there is, the higher the levels of happiness. So it's not about how much you make, as long as everyone makes about the same. But if some people make a lot more, it breeds unhappiness."

The reason getting more money doesn't make us happier, Emily, another Sparrow workmate who happened to be studying psychology, explained, is a phenomenon known as "hedonic adaptation."

"We get used to changes in our lifestyles, and when we get a bump in income, our expectations rise with it," she said. "All this, of course, happens subconsciously, which means we *can* become conscious in order to override it—if we so choose."

I mentioned that David Epstein, in his *Range Widely* newsletter, had an issue titled "Happiness Is a 2x2 Matrix." He cites the work of psychologists Robin Hogarth and Emre Soyer and their book *The Myth of Experience: Why We Learn the Wrong Lessons and Ways to Correct Them.* In the book they argue that happiness is a function of aligning what we have with what we want. When people are grateful, they are generally grateful for what they have.[4] They cite another psychologist, Hillel Einhorn, who constructed a matrix with "Have" and "Don't Have" on one axis and "Want" and "Don't Want" on the other. Most people understand that being grateful for what you have is helpful in not being envious, but Einhorn's matrix reveals that the largest alignment between our haves and wants is when we *don't have* what we *don't want.*[5] This has the potential to boost our gratitude. It's a variation on thinking of people who have it worse than you. And no matter how bad things are, there's always someone who has it worse.

We finished our beers and each made our separate ways home, thinking about this topic. I realized that's exactly what I'd spent the last four or so decades trying to do—make conscious within myself that which often otherwise remains unconscious.

Despite that work, though, I still fall subject to this consumeristic way of thinking. Through circumstances, I often find myself in groups of people with much higher incomes and seemingly more successful and rewarding lives. When people talk about taking their companies public, buying their third home or second jet, meeting the Queen of England, it's easy to start thinking about how little I have in comparison. Gratitude takes daily practice. It's like a muscle that must be worked or it will atrophy.

I have one hack that works for me; it's a list on my phone's Notes app called *When I'm Rich*. When I see something I want but can't really justify, even if I have the money, I put my desire on this list. The thought process is that, *Hey, if I get an unexpected windfall, then I might enjoy buying this.* This placeholder list keeps me from fixating on that which I do not have and thereby wasting a lot of time and energy.

As of right now, the list contains the following:

- Proper Cloth shirts: I love these amazing custom shirts, and already have a few, but then I start thinking I need/want more. They're always coming out with nice new fabrics and styles. The truth is, I have enough. I can wear only one shirt at a time, and I don't need that many. Still, I love putting ones I might like to buy on my list.

- Desk, monitor, etc.: I have a great office setup, but it would be nice to have an adjustable desk so I could stand up, and a bigger monitor, or two bigger monitors. Maybe a treadmill for underneath my desk so I could get some exercise during all those Zoom meetings. But do I need these things? Not really. I put them on my list, and if they continue to dog me, maybe I will eventually decide I want to buy them, but just keeping them on my list for a while allows space and openness around my desires.

- AirPods: Okay, I actually *did* get these. Francie and I are leaving for a trip to walk 450 miles on the Alpe Adria Trail in Europe. We will have some very long days of walking during which it would be nice to listen to books, music, or podcasts. The battery life on my old AirPods was diminishing, so yes, after they'd been on my list for some time I decided I needed these, though *need* is clearly a subjective word here.

- Rocky Mountaineer Trip: This train trip across Canada is something Francie and I have talked about for years. It's kind of like a cruise, but it's on a train instead of a ship and is not cheap if you get all the upgrades. Still, we take so many other types of trips that, while this different sort of adventure would be interesting, it's not going to break our hearts if we don't go, so for right now, it's in a holding mode. And to be honest, sometimes just imagining these things on my list is where I find the most joy. I don't have to possess my desires in order for them to blossom in my imagination.

> GRATITUDE TAKES DAILY PRACTICE. IT'S LIKE A MUSCLE THAT MUST BE WORKED OR IT WILL ATROPHY.

- Montbell Plasma 1000 Down Vest: On a recent hiking trip in Europe, I wanted to hedge my bets with a little more warmth if needed. Space was tight, so I put in my old Montbell vest that I've had for years. I unpacked it only a couple of times, and discovered it was way too large, so I'd be donating it when we returned home. It was a nice option to have, so at some point I may buy the Plasma 1000 version that is even lighter and more compressible and get it in the correct size for layering.

- iPhone mount for trekking pole: While I have pretty long arms that usually work well as a selfie stick, there are some situations where the ability for more reach could result in some better photos. When I used to use a digital camera, there was a great mount that just went on the bottom of a trekking pole, and I'm guessing there's something like that for an iPhone.
- Nitecore battery pack for Francie: I use the Nitecore NB10000 when traveling in Europe. On one trip, I had Francie bring an older, heavier one from my collection. I'm thinking it might be nice for her to have her own Nitecore battery. But we've been doing fine just using mine, so maybe just one is okay after all.
- *Masters of Change* book: This was recommended by David Epstein in his newsletter. It seemed interesting, but I have a stack of books to read already, so I'm not sure when I would get to this.

But, you ask, what's the point in denying myself these things if I can afford them and think I might enjoy them? Well, nothing. But then again, sometimes we maximize an experience by having less rather than having more.

My friend Mark Verber has what he calls a Shopping Diet, which is an evolution of my When I'm Rich list. He puts items he might want on the list, but he allows himself only two shopping windows a year. When those windows arrive, he goes through the list and either buys the item, removes it from the list, or leaves it on the list for now. He says that for him, 70 to 80 percent of the items either end up removed from the list or left on it to marinate.

So what *is* actually enough? This is where the lessons from ultralight backpacking come into play. When I'm in the wilderness to wander, I seek to minimize the weight of my pack for a number of reasons. First of all—and this was especially true when I worked a couple of jobs at a time and had limited time off—it allows me to maximize how much of the wilderness I can see in a limited time and lets me get farther into the backcountry. When your load is light enough to do twenty-five to thirty miles a day, you can cover a good bit of ground in a three-day weekend. A light pack allows me to make the most of my free time in the wilderness. As I get older, and my body is not as strong as it once was, a lighter pack still allows me to do long days, even if they're not as long as before.

ANOTHER REASON I LIKE TO MINIMIZE MY WEIGHT IS TO MINIMIZE THE THINGS THAT STAND BETWEEN ME AND NATURE.

Similarly at home, small efficiencies allow me to do more, especially more of what matters the most to me. One small example is when I'm in a shop that sells unique and interesting greeting cards. If I have time to browse, I'll buy a number of cards and then keep these hidden in my office. That way, when I'm thinking of Francie, I can write her a note and hide it somewhere, like on her pillow or in her car. If every time I thought I'd like to surprise her this way I had to stop, go to the store, find a card, buy it, come back and write it, it would not happen nearly as often. And even though Francie knows I buy lots of cards at a time, I still get credit for all the effort even when the actual time is only a fraction of that.

Another reason I like to minimize my weight is to minimize the things that stand between me and nature. Cowboy camping, for example, or sleeping under a simple tarp, places me right inside my surroundings rather than zipped inside a double-wall tent. Having a rudimentary shelter and a light sleeping bag forces me to be more conscious when selecting a campsite. Will I be protected from the wind? Will the cold air channel away from this location instead of settling here? If it rains, will the wetness pool underneath me or drain away? Will there be a breeze to keep mosquitos away, or will carpenter ants get to me, leaving silver dollar–size bruises on my armpits from their bites (true story!)?

From what I can see, it's all about consciousness, taking the time to think about these things and then making choices that enhance our lives—unlike that ill-begotten choice I made regarding my water consumption on the PCT between Tehachapi and Agua Dulce. I had been so concerned with weight and proving I could get my pack into the realm of such extreme lightness that I endangered my own health. We all do this, tipping the balance from carrying packs that are too light to ones that are too heavy, from engaging in too much stimulation in life to too little. In all aspects of our lives, balance matters, and it shapes what our ultimate experience will be. But to find our own true and unique balance, we have to first assess our choices.

Know Your Gear

"**THEY LEFT ME BECAUSE I WAS ONLY DOING TWENTY-MILE DAYS,**" the scraggly looking backpacker explained. He wore short shorts and carried what looked to be a simple daypack. He was skinny and dirty and didn't look to be in great shape. Read Miller and I were in the San Jacinto Wilderness with our Boy Scout troop, and we were all fascinated by him, stopping to share some of our food and drink.

"What's with the Ziploc bag of ramen behind your neck?" one of the boys asked.

"They took the group stove with them," he said of the two hiking pals who'd ditched him. "The only way I can cook now is with my own body heat."

"Dude!" the Scouts all said as one.

This happened during the time when I was still carrying a huge internal frame pack, and I tried desperately to wrap my head around the fact that he was hiking to Canada with that tiny pack, no stove, and logging twenty miles a day—far more than I could cover. At the time I didn't aspire to that level of lightness, but in the years that followed, I learned a lot about going light in the backcountry.

As an engineer, I created gear lists for every trip I undertook and refined my strategies over time to make things easier. In order to "take less" safely and effectively, you have to develop a foundational grasp of what you need to carry. The lesson "know your gear" works for more than just backpacking, but it is still critically important there. So that's what we're going to explore here. If you have no plans to be in the backcountry, you could skip this chapter altogether. But then again, like so much of what I've learned from ultralight backpacking, you may still find gems that inform some other part of your life, mined from hard-scrabble experience. In these pragmatic hacks, you never know where you'll find a treasure that may shift some element of your thinking in day-to-day life.

Ultralight Philosophy

In his intriguing book *Subtract*, Leidy Klotz lays out his arguments that we are all, as humans, wired to add rather than subtract, in essence to "take more" instead of "take less." His fascinating experiments, which started with Lego blocks and moved to editing music and writing, and finally more abstract grids, revealed a deep human bias to solve problems by adding as opposed to taking away. At biological, societal, and cultural levels, we have a tendency to overlook subtracting in favor of addition. Because of that bias, as humans it takes extra effort on our parts to be able to see options that solve problems by subtracting rather than by adding. In other words, it requires effort to see how "take less" can translate to "do more."

I'M AIMING TO TAKE LESS, WHICH WILL ALLOW ME TO DO MORE: HIKE MORE MILES, EXPLORE MORE TERRITORY, HAVE MORE FUN, MEET MORE CHALLENGES.

I have honed my gear and skills over the last forty years so they work well for me, although I'm always tinkering. The applicability of any of my gear and techniques to *your* situation will depend on a couple of things. My kit is geared toward trips that involve moving all day. I tend not to sit still well, and I like to see lots of wilderness, so I assume I'll be walking pretty much from sunrise (or a half hour before) until early evening or sunset. As such, I place a premium on gear weight since I spend all day carrying it. "Camp" for me generally just means where I sleep when it's dark enough that hiking becomes inconvenient. If you prefer to hike shorter days and spend more time around camp, you will likely make a number of gear choices that differ from mine.

When I evaluate my gear and processes, I'm looking for efficiency. I want to be safe, of course, and I want to be comfortable, but since I'm walking all day, the greatest comfort is a light pack. I'm aiming to take less, which will allow me to do more: hike more miles, explore more territory, have more fun, meet more challenges. I look to take the minimum amount of gear I need to be safe, assuming the generally expected conditions. When I can't find gear designed to that criteria, I create it. When designing gear, I assess materials and construction, evaluating their weight and the functions they need to serve. Much gear today is extremely overbuilt for its intended use, and there is often a trade-off between weight and durability. Using lighter gear means you need to take better care of it, understanding its limitations and making sure you don't ask the gear to perform outside of its intended range.

Often, using very light gear also means acquiring additional skills. Setting up an ultralight tarp usually requires a higher level of skill than setting up a traditional freestanding tent. Using a frameless pack effectively requires some packing and adjustment skills not necessary with heavy framed packs. Besides the setup or usage skills, more general proficiencies will also be required. When using a minimal sleeping bag, for example, choosing where to locate your campsite is crucial, as is understanding katabatic flows; that forethought can make the difference between a comfortable night and one that leaves you shivering until dawn. If you're not interested in or are unwilling to put in the work to acquire the additional skills, then you're better off carrying the additional weight.

As an engineer, I'm wired for problem-solving. So I would be lying if I didn't admit that part of the challenge, and joy, for me is seeing how light I can go. I know some people, referred to as "spreadsheet hikers," who spend countless hours working on the perfect gear spreadsheet and arguing on Reddit but who don't really get out backpacking that much. I actually do enjoy the trips and getting out into wilderness. But besides the majesty of mountain ranges and tranquility of alpine lakes, I enjoy the exercise of challenging myself.

Many backpackers are "packing their fears." If you are worried about being cold, you carry too heavy a sleeping bag or too many clothes. If your concern is being hungry, you will carry too much food. If bugs freak you out, you will carry a tent when a tarp might be sufficient. Past experience is helpful as a guide, but taking a sober look at the anticipated conditions and your current skill set before each trip is essential to reducing your pack weight. In the talks I give all over the world on lightening your load, I generally describe the process using these steps:

1. Know what your current gear weighs.
2. Look for multiple-use items.
3. Take less stuff.
4. Take lighter stuff.
5. Increase your knowledge and skills.

Now, let's look at a few specific areas where most people can reduce their pack weight, keeping in mind we're defining "base pack weight" as the total weight of your gear carried, not counting food and water or the clothes you're normally wearing.

Tent / Shelter / Bivy Sack / Hammock

I was in the High Sierra with a couple of friends under a tarp. We knew a storm would likely blow in overnight, so I positioned myself behind a huge boulder, thinking it would make a good windbreak and provide a degree of protection from the storm's full fury. The sandy decomposed granite soil on which I was camping was well drained. This was a stealth camp, and the ground was a steady, gentle grade, without any compacted depressions from years of people sleeping there. I used my trekking poles to set up the tarp and put rocks over the stakes to better anchor them as the soil became wet. Hours later, though, the trekking pole near my head vibrated so much that it was humming. The winds had shifted as the weather blew in and were now howling through my tarp, causing it to tremble uncontrollably. To prepare for what might happen next, I donned my headlamp and rain jacket and held my pack liner bag, ready to stuff my down sleeping bag into it if the storm were to rip the tarp from over my head. Then I just held on to the trekking pole to steady it. The stake at one corner of the tarp came loose, and I scampered out to find it (which is why I always tie a reflective line onto my stakes) and reset it, now with two rocks. I didn't get much sleep that night, but the shelter held through the rest of the storm, and we awoke to a glorious sunny morning.

While tents have gotten much lighter over the years, a tarp is significantly lighter still. Using a tarp will require additional ingenuity compared to setting up a typical freestanding tent and offers substantial weight savings, especially those constructed of DCF (Dyneema Composite Fabric, formerly Cuben Fiber), though a tarp is not ideal for every situation. To use a tarp effectively, you may need to learn something about knots, gain experience in site selection to take advantage of available natural protection, and get creative with different pitching options to deal with changing conditions. There are downsides, though. Tarps are suboptimal when there are a lot of bugs. If you're really hard core, you can put in ear plugs, take some Tylenol PM, and put on your head net, but I don't personally find this leads to a great night's sleep when bugs are plentiful. Also, depending on how the tarp is shaped and/ or pitched, it can be subject to splash during rainstorms. Some people like to use a bivy bag to compensate for splash off a tarp, but for me, the minimal weight solution is to have a large enough tarp so that the splash is far enough away not to get your sleeping bag wet, thus saving the weight of a bivy bag.

Hammocks have gained popularity, and the hammock of today is a far cry from the one of knotted nylon cord that I slept in while bicycling forty-two hundred miles across the country in 1976. They are lighter, more sophisticated in terms of entry and pitching, and more comfortable. I suspect hammocks are probably more comfortable compared to even an inflatable sleeping pad, depending on your sleeping style. Since I sleep fine on the ground with a ⅜" foam torso pad, carrying the weight of a hammock doesn't make sense to me, because you still have to address bugs and will still need a tarp to keep rain off if you anticipate either of those conditions. Also, since you may find yourself in the middle of sometimes cold air, you may need an "underquilt" or foam pad to provide insulation under the hammock.

Needless to say, you also need to find suitable trees to hang from. I'm sure, when you're a hammock person, you get good at spotting these, but since I enjoy a lot of my time above tree line, I've never been seriously tempted to try hammocks since my cross-country bike trek.

Sleeping System

We were up in the Sierra near Little Bear Lake in late fall. Humphreys Basin was a favorite haunt of mine when we lived in San Diego, and I have made many happy trips exploring the area west of Piute Pass. I have two custom sleeping bags, rated optimistically at 30°F and 20°F, respectively. On this trip, I had my 20°F bag as I knew it would be chilly. Since the night was clear, we were cowboy camping on the thick tufts of grass on a level spot above the lake. While I'm sure other people had camped there, there were no trails in the area and also no signs of previous occupation. I put my Western Mountaineering Flight down jacket on under my sleeping bag, along with pretty much all my other clothing. I woke during the night to check my Suunto watch, left near my head, for the temperature. When I took off my gloves, it felt very cold outside my jacket inside my down bag. Sure enough, it was 5°F outside.

No wonder my hands felt cold. I wouldn't say I was toasty, but thanks to my setup, I was able to pass the night without shivering (which has not always been true), so I counted it as a success.

Sleeping Bags

My bags are over twenty years old. There is now higher-lofting down, which can be treated to be water-resistant, as well as lighter fabrics and designs that weren't available when I had my bags made. Down has always been the lightest solution for sleeping bags. The reason some people eschew down is that when it gets wet, it provides no insulation, unlike synthetic insulation. But even before the advent of waterproof down, I had an experience that put my mind at ease. One night, in the snowy Beartooths, I was in a damp down bag, and overnight my body heat was enough to dry out the bag as I slept. After that, I no longer worried about a wet bag as much as I had when I was with the Boy Scouts. Sure, a dry sleeping bag is better, but a wet one doesn't mean I'm going to die.

Lots of people trade in their down sleeping bags for a quilt to save weight, and while I may be missing something, the math doesn't make sense to me, at least for my sleeping situation. Quilts may have some advantages, but I would argue that saving weight is not one of them.

The typical quilt seems to have some kind of toe box, and then an open bottom, with a strap system to attach it to your sleeping pad, and no hood. I get that it makes sense not having down underneath you, where the weight of your body compresses it and renders it essentially useless for insulation. And if you have a pad anyway, you don't really need that extra down. However, many quilts seem to be designed so that, when snugged up completely, basically the two sides almost butt up to each other on the bottom, negating the weight savings. Also, straps add weight with absolutely no insulation value.

My choice is a sleeping bag with no zippers, custom sewn by Nunatak back in the day, that likewise offers no down on the bottom. After a generous toe box, the bottom sixteen-inch width of the bag is a single piece of thin nylon. This accomplishes the goal of saving weight by not having down on the bottom, with the added benefits of no gaps for heat to escape—or for bugs or cold air to get in—and all without the hassle of straps. Besides, since I use a torso-length pad of ⅜" foam as a sleeping pad, it wouldn't provide the structure necessary to strap a quilt to. Still, it's perfect for slipping under my sleeping bag. And my sleeping bag has a well-insulated, integrated hood, which I find crucial for optimal insulation. Admittedly, since I no longer have significant hair on my head, I may be a little more sensitive to heat loss in this area than others.

STAYING WARM IN YOUR BAG ALSO INVOLVES SKILLS AND EXPERIENCE IF YOU WANT TO SAVE WEIGHT BY NOT CARRYING TOO HEAVY A BAG.

Ounce for ounce, for a given effective insulation value, I think an enclosed down bag with a single nylon layer on the bottom, no zipper, and a full hood is the clear winner. True, the benefit of an integrated hood and the attendant efficiencies does carry some drawbacks. While it's perfect for sleeping on your back, I, like many people, rotate all night between being on my back and on either side.

On my side, I've had to become adept at breathing out of one corner of the hood opening since it doesn't swivel. As far as I'm concerned, that's a fair trade-off for the thermal efficiency of an integrated hood, but others may come to different conclusions.

Staying warm in your bag also involves skills and experience if you want to save weight by not carrying too heavy a bag. It's important to make sure you're adequately hydrated and are fueling yourself with some fat content (nuts, nut butter, olive oil added to dinner, shortbread cookies) because that fat will take longer for your body to burn and help keep you warm longer. Plus, selecting a site that allows cold air, which gets denser as it cools, to drain away from you instead of pooling around you can make a huge difference in the ambient temperature. Likewise, adequately blocking breezes can help reduce convective heat losses. And, of course, wearing your puffy jacket, hat, and gloves will all help extend the temperature range of your bag. If I'm in my bag and I'm not wearing everything I have to keep warm, I either brought too many clothes or too warm a bag (or the temperatures were a lot warmer than anticipated!).

Sleeping Pads

Part of sleeping well, besides being warm enough, is being padded enough to be comfortable. If you're sleeping on nice sand, or a foot of forest duff, you really don't even need a pad, but for everything else, some kind of padding is necessary for most people. While technology has lowered the weight of inflatable sleeping pads, that makes them more susceptible to leaks and is thus the reason I avoid them. Still, many people ask how I stay comfortable on a 2.2-ounce foam pad.

My sleeping pad, made of ⅜-inch-thick foam that doubles as the pack frame in my pack, is 30 inches long, with a width of 16 inches at my shoulders and 12 inches at my waist, and this works perfectly for me. I find that the Evazote foam used in pads is incredibly light and a great insulator.

Before sleeping, though, I usually create what I call a GVP Divot by (1) choosing my sleeping area well and then (2) creating a small crater shaped for my butt. This will spread pressure evenly, supporting the small of my back and allowing me to sleep like a baby. But I only do this (and so should you) in a responsible Leave-No-Trace way, where you smooth back the sand or pine needles you displaced. The most comfortable night I ever had was when we camped in an area on the PCT in Southern California where the trail managers had been chipping the lower tree limbs. There was a thick bed of wood chips, and I got the divot just right. I drifted off and didn't wake up until the sun was streaming on my face.

Sometimes you're not in an area where you can create a divot. In those cases, I wad up a small piece of unused clothing. If you're not in bear country, food items or even trash in a double Ziploc can work. You toss this into your sleeping bag, then when you're lying down, position it in the small of your back. This serves the same purpose, supporting your spinal curve and spreading out the pressure of contact with the ground. When you turn on your side, simply move the wad so it's against your side, at your waist, and it will take some pressure off the hip. If you get good at this, the results are amazing.

Since most of the pressure is concentrated on your tailbone (when on your back, or on the hip if you're on your side), you can also cut a small foam circle and toss it in your bag to provide a double-thick pad at pressure points without carrying the weight of double thickness for the entire pad. Just adjust it when you're in your bag to the correct location, and you're good to go. You can even get fancy and cut a hole out of the middle (some have taken to calling this a "GVP donut") to better distribute weight off the pressure point. Keep in mind, sleeping is pretty much my super power, so your mileage may vary.

Finally, and not everyone will agree with this, but I find that a mild sleep aid can help take the edge off at night. I often use one to drift off to sleep, especially the first night or two when all the sounds are unfamiliar. And something like Tylenol PM or Ibuprofen PM can help ease the aches from a long, hard day of hiking. Medicate responsibly.

Pack

The group of three backpackers labored up the granite-chiseled steps alongside the north fork of Bishop Creek on their way to 11,400-foot Piute Pass and Humphrey's Basin beyond.

"How long are you going in for?" I asked them as they grunted under their towering packs.

"Three days," they wheezed as they struggled with both the elevation and the loads they were carrying.

"We did the same!" I said. "We're just finishing."

They stared at my lumbar pack, and I could tell that their oxygen-starved brains were simply unable to compute and too tired to inquire further.

And sure, while it wasn't the lightest solution possible, three days in the wilderness with just a lumbar pack was a fun experiment I'd been thinking about for a long time.

Since packs need to carry all your gear, they should be the last thing you reduce, but once you've minimized all your other gear, it's time to assess what you need to carry it.

My usual pack these days is the Gossamer Gear Murmur at 8 ounces. I've hiked with a 3.5-ounce pack but find that the Murmur strikes a nice balance of weight and function for most of my trips. It has a ton of helpful features, just with less weight than most other options. If you pack carefully and handle them carefully—and if they are designed to distribute weight to minimize stresses on that pack's materials—I find that most packs don't need to be constructed out of robust materials.

Of course, this obviously depends on your trip. If you're traveling two thousand miles in a remote area where the consequences of failure are severe, a more robust pack is probably worth the weight. Also, since my typical trailhead weight for a three-day trip is under twelve pounds, I don't generally use a waist belt. At those weights, a frame for weight transfer is also not really needed.

Compared to the days when I walked into REI to get packs for our son Brian and myself for a weeklong Boy Scout trip in the High Sierra, there are many lighter options today. I left the store back then with a newfangled internal frame pack that weighed over seven pounds completely empty. Today it's pretty easy to find full-featured packs, many including a frame and generously-padded shoulder straps and waist belts, that are under two pounds. You can select materials, capacity, and features based on your planned trips, your experience, and how light you've gotten the rest of your gear.

When people ask me, "How big a pack do I need?" my response is always the same: "That's the wrong question. Ask yourself how small a pack can you get away with." Large packs give you room to take more and do less.

Food/Cooking

I was high up in the Southern California PCT with our then thirteen-year-old son Grant, preparing dinner before descending the next day into Agua Dulce. Grant liked pizza more than anything else at this point in his life, and in fact pizza may have constituted more than half of the calories he ingested on a weekly basis. Despite the fact I was cooking at this time on a small alcohol stove made out of a Pepsi can, I had a surprise for him that night. I took out a Boboli crust and small bags of tomato paste and shredded cheese. With a piece of folded aluminum foil, I proceeded to make an ersatz oven over the small burner. That night, we enjoyed warm "pizza" with melted cheese before snuggling into our sleeping bags.

After a long day of hiking, there's nothing that soothes body and soul like a good meal. This is true at home too. When there have been daily challenges or strife, a delicious meal makes all the difference. This is why people bring casseroles to those who have been sick or are in the throes of grief. Caring for ourselves and each other in this very elemental way does more than provide calories to the bodies that need them; it refreshes the lagging spirit as well. And though our goal, if we're going ultralight into the backcountry, is to do so with as little weight as possible, there's no need to skimp on this very essential part of what gives pleasure to any trip: food that's been well planned and nourishes both body and soul.

That said, food is one area, believe it or not, where most of us can stand to lose some pack weight. To do so, I tend to focus on two key elements.

One: I make sure the food I select contains a reasonable amount of calories for the weight. For instance, I make sure that all food items I carry provide a minimum of 100 calories per ounce. One way to juice this calorie content is to include calorie-dense items like nuts or to bring a packet of olive oil to stir into your dinners. Ryan Jordan, cofounder of Backpacking Light, once told me about an Arctic trip where one of the choice foods on offer were sticks of butter rolled in brown sugar. Who knows: in that environment, that might be really tasty!

FOOD IS ONE AREA, BELIEVE IT OR NOT, WHERE MOST OF US CAN STAND TO LOSE SOME PACK WEIGHT. TO DO SO, I TEND TO FOCUS ON TWO KEY ELEMENTS.

Two: I'm careful not to take too much. Before I go, I create lists and strategies. I plan on consuming between 1.2 and 1.4 pounds of food per day. Dinner, for me, tends to be heavier, so I adjust the total day count accordingly. For instance, if I'm trying for 1.4 pounds per day, and the first day I'll have breakfast before we start, I'll figure on 1.1 pounds for the rest of that day. Likewise, if the last day means we'll be back to civilization before dinner, I might figure that day at 0.8 pounds or so. It's kind of funny, but I find that on more relaxed, easier trips, I tend to eat more than I do on the more strenuous treks when every calorie counts. Either way, I pay strict attention to the weight, because—well, what else is there but weight when you're a geek like me?

But I also know from experience that if I pack more than about 1.4 pounds per day, I'll end up bringing food back with me. I know I've planned just right, as Goldilocks would have said, if I come off the trail with no food left and feeling a bit hungry, with a PROBAR waiting for me in the car.

As mentioned earlier, I prefer to eat a plant-based diet, so this inclination also affects my food choices. I make some exceptions for backpacking, though, mostly by taking packs of string cheese for lunch because I like the taste and nutrition, and they keep well in the heat. My buddy Read Miller did an experiment, leaving a package of string cheeses in the trunk of his car during the summer and taking one out weekly to eat. He never got sick, so he concluded that string cheese is pretty stable for backpacking, though you might want to consult a health professional before taking food advice from a hiker.

Variety is key to avoid boredom, and by nature, food choices are largely a matter of personal taste. So you will want to individualize everything to focus on what appeals the most to you.

I don't bundle up complete packages per day, as some hikers do. I prefer to make selections as I go so I'm eating what most appeals to me in the moment. To make this easy, I use thin plastic produce bags from the grocery store to group similar items together: all the breakfasts in one bag, same for lunches, dinners, snacks. (In the early days, Read and I used the standard plastic grocery bags to carry food. Compared to a stuff sack, it's easier to open and see what's inside. I eventually sewed a bag from spinnaker fabric in the same pattern, and this is what I use now.) This system simply makes it easier to find the meal I'm looking for rather than digging through all kinds of random food in my bag. I keep my snacks packaged in small daily portions so I can drop one into a pocket and reach it throughout the day.

Breakfast

Since I carry minimal insulation for sleeping at night, I like to get up and get moving first thing in the morning. I want to get my blood moving to warm me just as the dawn is breaking. This strategy also minimizes the amount of clothing I have to carry since I don't need the added insulation for sitting around in camp in the cold morning air.

Typically in the morning before setting out, I'll pull out my breakfast for that day along with maybe a bar and some small energy gel packets; I'll put those items in the pocket of my pack. Then I'll take one of my small Ziploc bags filled with snacks and put it into a pants pocket for easy access. I'll get into my food bag later during lunch and dinner, but I don't worry about that first thing in the morning. And since my hiking style favors movement over sitting, this way I'm all geared to keep snacking without having to stop. If I'm particularly hungry, maybe I'll gnaw on half a PROBAR as I walk, but generally I can go a few hours without eating.

After a couple of hours of hiking, I'll find a nice sunny spot for a more leisurely breakfast, taking out a small Ziploc bag in which I've put the following ingredients:

- ¾ cup or so of Grape-Nuts cereal
- ¼ cup of dried fruit bits (blueberries, pomegranate seeds, and cherries are my favorites; I keep them in different bags so I can adjust for variety)
- 3 Tbsp powdered coconut milk (for calories, also lends a nice taste)
- 2 Tbsp brewer's yeast (a rich source of minerals, protein, and B-complex vitamins)
- 2 Tbsp powdered almond or soy milk (or, if unavailable, powdered whole milk or goat milk).

When it's time for this midmorning breakfast, I'll pour water into the Ziploc bag, fold down the top for easy access, and happily spoon out the tastiness. Or, if I didn't feel like making this mixture when I was preparing for this outing, I'll have a snack bag of granola ready to go, the kind from the bulk bins at the health food store with the largest clusters for ease of eating. Or, I might have what I think of as a breakfast quesadilla, a stick of string cheese wrapped in a good-quality flour tortilla.

If I'm hiking with a group of people and they actually want to cook breakfast, I'll treat myself to an instant coffee. Starbucks Via is easy to source, but there are other great options, like C&S Coffee and Black Rifle Coffee. Sometimes I take cold water from my Smart Water bottle, add an instant coffee packet, shake it, and enjoy some cold coffee in the morning. Most times, to avoid stopping, I'll munch on a handful of dark chocolate–covered espresso beans as I hike for a little morning buzz.

Lunch

I favor a stick of string cheese and maybe a vegan jerky strip, like Primal Strips or Louisville Vegan Jerky. To mix it up, I might squeeze a package of Trail Butter on flavored Triscuit crackers or other hard-tack kind of bread. Three ounces of crackers per day seems about the right amount. I've also used tortillas, and crispbreads can be good, though Triscuits tend to be my go-to. They're easy to find, travel well with minimal breakage, and come in different flavors to keep the taste buds excited. Depending on the trip, sometimes a cold-soak salad from Outdoor Herbivore is a nice break.

Snacks

If, as they say, variety is the spice of life, it's important to not get tired of what you pack to eat. Like I found on the desert portion of the Pacific Crest Trail, if water doesn't appeal, I won't stop to drink, and if the food doesn't whet my appetite, I'll soon be in trouble with not enough calories to fuel me. To keep the taste buds happy and interested with what's on offer, I almost always bring small snack

Ziploc bags of either Chex Party Mix or Cheez-It Snack Mix. There's something about the different textures and spices that's highly satisfying. I eat a small bag every day I'm on the trail and have done so for years. Sometimes I'll also take Clif shot blocks, or something similar, enjoying one or two a day as a little treat. I may also bring nuts or a PROBAR or two when I can fit them into the weight limit. The taste and food value is awesome (plus they are vegan), and they have a lot of flavors to keep my mouth intrigued. One friend, Henry Shires of Tarptent, always lugs a huge bag of flavored sesame snacks. I've been meaning to copy that idea, but I keep forgetting.

I also carry Emergen-C powdered drink. I mix it weak, and generally consume three to four packets a day, in a liter of water each. I use a one-liter Smart Water bottle for this purpose so as to keep the tube on my hydration bladder for water alone, thus making sure it doesn't get gunked up. While living in San Diego, I would often be hiking in heat and regularly traversed from sea level, where I lived, to high altitudes. As long as I stuck to my Emergen-C regimen, I wouldn't get cramps or stiffness despite long days of high mileage on an aging body that generally didn't get much exercise between trips. I turned Ron Moak of Six Moon Designs on to Emergen-C and was rewarded with a grateful video from his Continental Divide hike, saying it was a game changer.

Dinner

For dinner, I've followed a simple strategy for many years. I start with three to four ounces of dry food, like instant potatoes, couscous, dried black bean flakes, instant rice, freeze-dried lentils, dehydrated sweet potatoes, quinoa flakes, or polenta. To that, I add one and a half or two ounces of an olive-oil-based sauce I made ahead of time with a variety of spices.[6]

Before I discovered this technique, I never really looked forward to dinner, but with these recipes, dinner is a high point of every day. The flavors are awesome, especially with some experimentation on the sauces, and the olive-oil-and-salt base keeps very well in hot climates. I make up my sauce batches at the beginning of the season and store them in small plastic water bottles in the back of the refrigerator at home in a spot my wife doesn't look. I'll also measure out my dry ingredients into Ziploc bags and store them in a cool, dry place. This way, to prepare for a trip, it's a simple matter of decanting the appropriate amount of sauce into a small squirt bottle and grabbing a couple of my premixed dry bags. Before I add my sauce bottles to my pack, I always encase them in a pint freezer Ziploc bag to avoid spills.

THOSE LAST MILES OF THE DAY ARE USUALLY EASY BECAUSE I'M CHARGED UP FROM A GOOD DINNER AND THE DAY HAS COOLED OFF. I OFTEN GET TO ENJOY THE WILDLIFE STARTING TO BECOME ACTIVE.

It's sometimes nice to add enhancements to the dry ingredients. Depending on the meal, I might throw in pine nuts, dried mushrooms, sun-dried tomatoes, even freeze-dried tofu (or for an omnivore, some meat), all of which can provide flavor and/or protein. A favorite, which I picked up from Brian Frankle (founder of ULA), is Frito bits. I buy a small bag of Fritos, stick a pin in it to let the air out, then crush the Fritos to bits for easier packing, putting a piece of tape over the pinhole to preserve the freshness. Stirring Frito bits in at the end of cooking adds a calorie-rich crunchy treat, excellent with potatoes, rice and beans, and sweet potatoes. Brian also uses Funyuns in a similar manner.

My dinners are weighted with fat calories, which helps keep me warm at night with the minimal clothing, sleeping bag, and pad I carry. Sometimes, to provide my muscles some extra protein at night for recovery, I add a protein bar as a dessert. There are a lot of bad-tasting ones out there, but I like the Stinger, Raw Revolution, or PROBAR ones best; they really taste like dessert.

When I'm going through a lazy stretch and don't feel like working much to plan my meals, I use prepackaged dehydrated meals for dinners and sometimes a cold-soak one for lunch.

If hiking by myself, I often prefer not to eat dinner at my campsite but to make my final meal of the day in the late afternoon/early evening, then hike on for a while before setting up camp. This allows me to pick a dinner spot for its beauty and water availability. It doesn't have to be a good camping spot and I don't need a lot of extra insulation because the chill of the day hasn't set in yet. That way, once I make it to my campsite, my workload is reduced since I don't have to cook dinner, and I won't be emitting cooking smells in camp that might attract the attention of bears or other varmints.

Those last miles of the day are usually easy because I'm charged up from a good dinner and the day has cooled off. I often get to enjoy the wildlife starting to become active. That's really what it's all about, enjoying the backcountry.

Cooking System

I cook in a pot fashioned from a Heineken can, supported by a Trail Designs Caldera, using solid fuel tabs (either Esbit or Bleuet). For some dry items, like instant potatoes and couscous, I just pour hot water into the freezer Ziploc, stir it up, and eat—no need to wait. Most "add boiling water" meals require some rehydration time. My current routine when not in bear country is to roll up to a campsite; pull my tarp, food bag, and clothing bag out of my pack; and get my cooking pot going. Then, in the eight minutes or so it takes to boil water, I set up my shelter. Coming back to the stove, I pour the now boiling water into my dinner, stir to mix, and place it in my fluffed-up sleeping bag, now the only thing in my pack. Then I will add a little more water to the pot and heat for a few more minutes, adding some instant miso soup powder. I'll put the pot with miso soup back into the insulated stuff sack and enjoy sipping on the soup as evening deepens and my dinner rehydrates. By the time I finish my soup and clean out the pot and repack the windscreen, dinner is ready. I put the hot bag into the insulated stuff sack to keep it warm and enjoy my hot dinner. The last bite of the dinner is still hot, and thanks to the stuff sack, it's easy to hold without burning my hands. This system is simple and nice with minimal cleanup. Others may use a Jetboil or MSR Pocket Rocket and a titanium pot. I admit my system isn't as fast as those, but it's a lot lighter, and if you plan accordingly, the extra time is not wasted. If you've ever listened to a Pocket Rocket at full blast, the noiseless flame of a fuel tablet is a nice change.

I hike with some people who have opted for not cooking at all. Typically they "cold soak" meals, often in a Talenti gelato container. There are some commercial cold-soak meals, but it's easy to make your own with ingredients from bulk bins at your local health food store. There's definitely some weight savings, even over my minimal system. And there's the sheer simplicity of it, nothing to go wrong, no stove to break, no wet matches or broken lighter to deal with. I always say, cold soak sounds like a great idea until everyone else is cooking.

Then again, you could split the difference between stove and cold soak. To this end, I was so inspired by the hiker with the ramen behind his neck that I invented what I call the "crotch pot," a stove-less way of preparing a meal. This "invention" came about on a hike I did with other founders of ultralight equipment companies. There was Ron Moak from Six Moon Designs, Henry Shires of Tarptent, Brian Frankle of ULA Designs, and me. We jokingly called it the Brain Trust hike and figured that if all four of us perished in some event, it would've been a serious setback to ultralight backpacking at the time. These trips were always filled with lively discussions and some trash-talking, and somehow the topic of using body heat to warm food came up. Never one to miss an opportunity, I took a Ziploc bag, put in my dinner and some water, and tucked it into my pants, folding the top over my waistband to keep it from sliding down too far. When I went to check on it, the top ripped and I narrowly avoided wearing my dinner in my pants.

We all laughed, but at Gossamer Gear, we later perfected the design and debuted the Crotch Pot on an April Fool's Day.

It's true, though. Infrared images of the human body confirm what is basically common knowledge: one of the hottest parts of the human body is the crotch area. Plus, your body naturally generates significant heat while hiking, and so I wondered, *Why not harness this heat for a warm dinner while also saving the weight and hassle of cooking?* On the days I plan to use this technique, I add cold water to the dry ingredients in my Ziploc bag and slip the bag into my pants, directly next to my skin for best results. I hike on for the final hour or so, kneading the meal (discretely) while walking to make sure things are mixing well; sometimes I have to add additional water. When I get to camp, I simply pull out my dinner, grab my spoon, and enjoy!

This works well for breakfast too. When you break camp, slip a bag of hydrated instant oatmeal into your pants, and when the sun comes out after a few miles, enjoy a warm breakfast without the hassle of breaking out a stove and pot to boil water.

First Aid

My friend Will Rietveld and I were high in the Weminuche Wilderness in Colorado, off trail. Will is as spry as a mountain goat despite being my senior by fifteen years, and he makes me look like a heavyweight packer. He knows the Weminuche better than most people know their local park. We were negotiating a course across a talus field when Will slipped and gashed his leg on a sharp boulder. Because of his lightweight pack, his only first aid supplies were two Band-Aids and the duct tape wrapped around his trekking pole. He applied these to his wound, but after a short time it was obvious from the amount of blood seeping through that these were not sufficient.

I dug into my kit, debrided and cleaned the wound, added antibiotic ointment, closed the gash with suture strips, and added a Tegaderm bandage to seal it. We continued to hike and he figured he'd need to have it tended to professionally when we got back to Durango. As it turned out, it healed so well he never bothered.

A first aid and emergency kit is an essential piece of gear for any backcountry excursion. While it may seem like an easy place to cut weight in your pack, it's important to balance that desire with the realities of the trail. While you may never use some pieces of your kit, you may come across another person who needs the items. At the minimum, these kits can help soothe your hot spots, but in more serious circumstances they can save a life. After decades of light-weight backpacking experience, I have figured out what I consider to be the perfect minimal but essential first aid kit. (For gear lists, first aid items list, and more information, see the appendix.)

I don't often get blisters, but Omnifix or Kinesio tape are great for treating hot spots before they get to the blister stage. If that doesn't do it, the Compeed strips with their gel pads are usually great. You stick them on and, if the area is clean and dry, they will stay on for days protecting the blister. As I hike with other older people like myself, I appreciate that our skin is thinner and more fragile, so scrapes can bleed profusely. Suture strips and Tegaderm bandages, as I discovered with Will, are great to fix up large cuts from grazing sharp talus.

Because I am prone to fever blisters, especially with the sun and exertion that come with backpacking, I carry Valtrex, a prescription medicine. When I lived at sea level, it was also common to feel touches of altitude sickness on the first day of a trip in the Sierra, so I carried Excedrin. It includes caffeine, which, assuming you drink lots of water with it, helps rebalance the pH of your blood and relieves the altitude symptoms. Tylenol PM helps me get to sleep the first couple of nights of a trip, until I adapt to nights on the ground.

I store these first aid items in a tough four-by-six-inch storage bag, currently the Smelly Proof brand.[7] I have had to wade streams and don't use a pack cover, so I want to know that my first aid and emergency supplies will stay together and dry. I tend to group things within the kit so that I can quickly get to items I need without having to search through the entire kit.

Over the last few years, I've taken to ordering the medications from minimus.biz, so they come in individually labeled packets. I used to just put a few pills in a mini Ziplock, cutting out the tiny cardboard piece from the box that includes the medication name and then writing the expiration date on the back. My thinking was that if I'm incapacitated or someone else is trying to use my first aid kit, they will be able to tell what everything is.

For anything I use on a trip, I now leave the wrappers in the kit. When I get home, I unpack and replenish the used items so it's always ready to go. Typically, at some point during the winter when I'm not backpacking, I'll go through and check expiration dates and order any new supplies I need to have on hand for resupply between trips.

My first aid kit has remained fairly constant over the years, although there's been some refinement. It's geared toward trips of a week or less because those are the trips I take. For a thru-hike, I make adjustments. I'm not a medical professional and have no special training other than a Wilderness Advanced First Aid course I took a number of years ago. The contents are based on issues I've encountered on trips over the past two decades. Apart from the Tylenol PM and the Excedrin, I rarely use any of it personally. A more likely case is in helping other people on a trip. Funny enough, I often end up helping folks who are carrying a much more substantial kit themselves, but they just don't happen to have the one item that they need. I could certainly lighten it up a lot, but most of the items have come in useful for treating other people.

Like much of ultralight backpacking, one's skills play an important role. Not just skills in treating wounds and common backcountry maladies but also experience in planning and executing a trip so you don't get into trouble in the first place. As the expression goes, any time you head into the wilderness, you're "three bad decisions away from not coming back."

When you review reports of people who perished in the backcountry, it's typically a cascading series of errors in judgment. Doing proper research on the route, preparing for the anticipated weather conditions, and being certain of the fitness level and expertise of your companions can all be crucial. Making sure that the demands of the trip are within your experience level will help keep you out of trouble and ensure you return safely to plan the next trip.

Putting It All Together

Even once you've selected and winnowed the gear you take, it's worth giving some thought to how you pack it. The type of adventure will dictate this in different ways. The points I consider when selecting the location for packing gear include the following:

- The weight of the gear. Heavier gear for backpacking is often best carried high, whereas for bike-packing it's nice to have the weight low for stability.
- The bulk of the gear. In backpacking, how it fits in the pack to maximize use of the space is important with a small pack. Also, with things like a down sleeping bag, it's nice to have a system that allows the bag not to be compressed too much, to preserve the effectiveness of the bag. For bikepacking, where you have smaller compartments and more of them, the volume of items becomes an important consideration in terms of what will fit where.
- How often I'm going to need an item. Things like sunscreen or water filtration, which I'm going to use multiple times in the day, I'll want to keep more accessible than my cooking kit, which I'm going to pull out only once.

- When in the day I'm going to need an item. Something that I'm going to need at lunch I want to have more easily accessible than something that I'm not going to access until the end of the day.
- How quickly I'm going to want to be able to lay my hands on an item. This may trump previous considerations about how often and when. I don't expect to access my first aid kit during a typical trip. But if there's an accident and I *do* need it, I want to be able to get to it quickly. I usually don't access my Garmin InReach until sending a message at the end of the day. But if conditions change and I need to get a message out sometime during the day, I don't want to be digging through the bottom of my bag looking for it. A spoon is another example. I may not plan on using my spoon until the end of the day at dinner, but I've found sometimes opportunities present themselves where someone has, for instance, too much ice cream and wants to share, so I like to keep my spoon handy to capitalize on these opportunities if they occur.

AS THE EXPRESSION GOES, ANY TIME YOU HEAD INTO THE WILDERNESS, YOU'RE "THREE BAD DECISIONS AWAY FROM NOT COMING BACK."

Efficiency in Hiking

While your goals may differ, one of my goals in the wilderness is to explore more territory. If you're hiking point-to-point on a long trail, how many miles a day you do between resupply points will impact the amount of food weight you have to carry. For these reasons, it may be useful to consider efficiency in hiking.

If you've ever been hiking with someone and stopped to put on sunscreen or something similar, you've likely been struck by how far ahead the person you were hiking with is now ahead of you. While certainly your stride and cadence will affect your hiking speed, one of the most effective ways to cover ground is to be always moving, or as close to that as you can get. If you spend time hiking behind thru-hikers, you'll notice all sorts of tricks in their gaits—stepping over log steps instead of on top of them, scanning ahead so they can hop rocks to cross a stream with no hesitation, even figuring out what photo they want to take, pulling out their phone as they approach the spot, and snapping a pic, barely breaking stride. They are ruthlessly efficient in their strides but also in minimizing their stops.

The shorthand for efficient hiking is "constant forward motion." It's about minimizing stops and maintaining a pace by planning steps ahead through constant scanning of the trail. When I'm hiking by myself, I think of things that I need to do, like applying sunscreen and taking off a jacket, so I can "batch" them, minimizing stops. Every time I stop and take off my pack, I want to get everything done I can.

With proper planning, it's surprising how much you can do without taking off your pack or even stopping. I've hiked behind someone as she pretty much changed outfits without ever stopping. Most thru-hikers can take off a jacket and stow it in their pack without ever stopping walking (depending on the trail, of course). With the right water bottle setup, you don't need to stop to get a drink. I carry items I want ready access to—snacks, sunscreen, water treatment, bandanna, reading glasses, map, phone—in my pockets so I don't need to stop walking to access them. Part of being efficient is thinking ahead. *What conditions am I likely to experience in the next few hours, and what will I need for them?* When I pull up to a water source, I can simply pull my water bottle out of my side pocket and fill it without ever removing my pack. If it needs treatment, I pull a mini bottle of bleach out of a pants pocket to add a few drops. Within minutes, I'm back on the trail. If the water source is shallow, I have a Ziploc bag at the ready (marked to also serve as a measuring cup) to scoop out water without disturbing sediment on the bottom.

Thru-hiker efficiency also extends to camp. Many years ago, I was hiking on the Appalachian Trail with Larry "the Salesman." He had hiked over ten thousand miles at that point. I considered myself pretty efficient and focused, but the Salesman was always a half step ahead of me, and I never saw him hurry. Whenever I finished something and looked up, he was already halfway through the next task. To get more efficient in hiking, a sure way is to hike with people who have hiked many more miles than you.

In Closing

As you work to lighten your pack load, I have a couple of final suggestions. First is that you make changes gradually. To avoid getting into trouble, never reduce your pack in excess of your compensating experience. Much of going lighter is about gaining experience, which is best done gradually to make sure it's survivable.

Play around with new gear at home so you know how to use it before you head into the wilderness. There's nothing like pulling out a new tarp or tent in the middle of a storm above tree line to find out that it doesn't have stakes or a ground sheet and that you need to knot and attach all the guylines while being soaked by rain.

Find other friends who are also lightening their packs so you're not shackled with people still carrying loads too heavy for the things you want to do. Or, better yet, help your existing friends to lighten their packs as you learn. Be a resource for others who are interested. To supercharge the process, find people with lighter packs than you and go backpacking with them.

And if you're *not* a backpacker, think about how Leidy Klotz's work shows how we're wired to add rather than subtract to solve problems, and think how you might possibly solve the next problem (or opportunity for improvement) you have by using less instead of more.

do more

LESSON 8

Invest in Relationships

AS WE HAVE SEEN BY NOW, "TAKE LESS" SO THAT ONE CAN "DO more" has been a life theme for me—and not just when it comes to ultralight backpacking. When my life is encumbered with things, tasks, burdens, and anything else that weighs me down, I accomplish less. I become too busy to get to the "more" of life. The more unencumbered I am, the more freedom I have to do what I want to do. Because of this philosophy, I have tried to scrutinize my life in the same way I scrutinize my backpack: to make sure I am not carrying too much or figure out how I can lighten the load of the things I need to carry.

This is a much harder task than lightening a backpack. As a habitual workaholic, finding this balance has taken a lot of effort. And when it comes to the first lesson of "doing more"—invest in your relationships—I had a traumatic experience earlier in my marriage that seared this lesson into me.

Rick was in the copilot's seat, and Dave, the pilot, was next to him. I was seated behind Rick, looking over his shoulder as he snoozed, watching Dave's flying. I had my own private pilot's license, and earlier, Dave and I had geeked out together over flying stuff, comparing planes we'd flown, instruments we loved and hated, our favorite small-time airports. Now, as I looked out the cockpit window and we sailed through the night, everything was quiet and calm.

Sean was seated next to me, and Bill was in the back. By this time of the evening, most everyone on the plane, other than Dave and me, was napping. It had been a big weekend.

The five of us had flown from northern Orange County, near where we all lived, to a private ranch near Clearlake in Northern California to attend a capstone weekend for an all-men's personal development seminar we'd been enrolled in. This event included breakout sessions on healing one's own trauma, understanding better how human psychology often mucked up relationships, and learning to be a better leader of self. I had loved every moment of the time away. I was always looking for ways to grow as a human—a legacy from my mom—striving to be as awake as possible, to live up to my potential. I listened to cassette tapes and read self-help books by Brian Tracy, Napoleon Hill, Og Mandino, Norman Vincent Peale, Dale Carnegie, and Stephen R. Covey. I wanted to live my life to its fullest and make the best contribution I could. Some of the men on this plane I had known before getting involved in this personal development group, and some I had met along the way. I wasn't super close with any of them, but we had some shared experiences that created a bond.

As a treat to us, and to get more pilot hours, Dave had offered to rent this private plane to fly us there and back, a kind of celebration of the work we were doing in developing ourselves. On the way down the coast, we'd stopped in San Francisco and gone to Fisherman's Wharf for a delicious seafood dinner, toasting each other, glad to be in each other's company. We'd grown closer over the weekend and all felt determined to continue making our lives as meaningful as possible once we got home.

Chief among the plans in my book was to make sure I demonstrated to Francie and our young son Brian how much I appreciated them. As I have said, I tended to be a workaholic and kept my nose to the grindstone, focusing solely on my work while sometimes the world blew to smithereens around me without my notice. That attitude had saddled Francie with a lot of responsibility. I needed to open my aperture more, be more cognizant of the people in my life, and be certain I showed them how much they meant to me by paying attention to their struggles and needs. We were expecting our second child in a few months, and I wanted to be sure our family foundation was as firm as possible before that magnificent event occurred. Did they know how much they meant to me? I worried that I had not shown Francie how important she was to me. I realized that I needed to correct this.

As we flew through the night skies above the city lights of Orange County, I was looking over Rick's shoulder and watching Dave's movements. Suddenly the shrimp and scallops in my stomach from our Fisherman's Wharf dinner became heavy. The engine stuttered, and I saw Dave shift from the right wing fuel tank to the left, tapping into what he assumed was our remaining fuel reserve. Earlier, though, I'd seen him shift from the left tank to the right, which meant that he was now switching to a tank that was already empty. He was hoping against hope that we somehow had enough fuel remaining to power us to our intended destination, John Wayne Airport. We didn't. We were on vapors.

The reality of what was happening slammed me. This was not going to end well. Poor Francie. If I died in this plane, I'd be leaving her a widow with a toddler and a soon-to-be newborn. How had this happened? The engine coughed again and now Dave also knew we were in trouble.

"Find the nearest airport," he said, thrusting the Jeppesen at me since he knew I had my pilot's license, while he concentrated on adjusting trim and putting the plane into a glide. The Jeppesen was a ringed binder with pages for all the airports in the region containing their radio frequencies, coordinates, and other vital information. I knew the area well enough to know we were near Meadowlark Airport, about a mile east of the Pacific Ocean in Huntington Beach. We were going to have to make an emergency landing there.

"What's the frequency?" Dave asked, keeping his voice calm so as not to rouse the others from their slumber and alarm them as he directed the plane, powerless now, toward the little airport.

"I'm looking! It should be right here! Are the pages out of order?" I kept flipping, searching alphabetically. Nothing.

"What's the frequency?!" He was getting more agitated.

Meadowlark is a tiny airport with houses built all around it. Because residents had complained of the airport's light pollution, the airport had agreed to keep the lights off except when needed. A pilot would have to change his transponder to a particular frequency and then click his mic to turn on the runway lights. That frequency was what I was hunting for in the Jeppesen. It wasn't there.

MY ENTIRE BODY SHOOK WITH THE VIOLENCE OF THE CRASH, BUT ONCE THE HEADACHE-INDUCING NOISE SUBSIDED, I COULD HEAR MY OWN HEARTBEAT DRUM IN MY EARS. THAT BLESSED HEARTBEAT. I WAS ALIVE!

We needed those lights to see the runway. Without them, we were pretty well flying blind. But I couldn't locate the Meadowlark listing. I kept leafing through the binder, my hands sweating and my breath ragged. Where was it?

By now, we were slowly losing altitude, flying over the beach city with absolutely no thrust. What I had forgotten in the stress of the moment was that there are two different sections in the Jeppesen, one for "controlled" airports with a tower and one for "uncontrolled," those without a tower, like Meadowlark. Later I realized I had been looking in the "controlled" section, which was why there was no listing for Meadowlark.

Not that it mattered at this point, because we were about to crash-land. I braced myself as I'd been taught, my head against the back of my hands, which were positioned along Rick's seatback. This might be it. How stupid of me to lose my life as the result of a weekend meant to enhance my life. I thought of the founder of the program we'd just attended. He'd died in a private plane crash, leaving his wife and others involved in the movement to carry on with his work. Was I about to do the same to Francie?

As the earth came up to meet us, Dave somehow managed to miss all the little homes that surrounded the airport. Before I knew what was happening, though, a huge roar thundered in my ears, blotting out everything else, including the blaring stall warning. Glass and metal were breaking everywhere, steel twisting out of shape and screaming in resistance. I would find out later that we skidded through a grove of eucalyptus trees, shearing off both wings in the process, ripping them cleanly from the fuselage. I don't know if I lost consciousness, only that the sound was so loud, it kept ringing in my ears for what seemed an eternity, a shrill shrieking of metal torsion that took up residence inside my eardrums.

My entire body shook with the violence of the crash, but once the headache-inducing noise subsided, I could hear my own heartbeat drum in my ears. That blessed heartbeat. I was alive!

As the sound inside and out slowly began to lessen, I felt my body. I seemed to be okay. My head was bleeding from where my watch had imprinted itself on my forehead. I hurt all over in a general way but otherwise felt intact apart from shaking in shock. But what about the others?

I called out to the rest of the guys. "Rick. Bill. You okay? Sean?" No one answered. As far as I knew at this point, I was the sole survivor of the crash. I could see Rick in front of me was hurt.

His seat had come off its track and he'd smashed into the front of the cockpit, breaking every bone in his face, I'd later learn. He was unconscious. I got myself out of the plane—easy enough now that there was no longer a door; it had been blown off in the impact. I stood on the ground and tried to figure out what I needed to do next. My legs were like jelly, and I was in shock.

Were they dead or just unconscious? I didn't know. My first instinct was that I needed to get them away from the plane in case it was about to explode, figuring that was more important than not moving them to avoid exacerbating internal injuries. I hadn't factored in that there was no fuel left to combust; clearly, I wasn't thinking rationally. I was barely holding my own body up and didn't know how I was going to get the others out. But I did, somehow. I was able to get Rick from the copilot's seat and laid him on the ground as the sound of sirens filled the night. Soon, the first responders took over extricating the rest of the passengers and I found myself ushered into an ambulance. I don't remember much of what happened from that point on—I think I passed out on the way to the hospital—but I worried about how Francie would take the news. Later, she told me about the call.

"This is Huntington Beach Hospital. There's been a plane crash involving your husband. You need to go to the hospital. And bring a friend."

"Is he alive?" she'd asked.

"I can't tell you anything. Just get to the hospital with a friend."

She was six months pregnant at the time. Quickly, she found someone to stay with two-year-old Brian and someone else to drive her to the hospital in the middle of the night on a mission to learn if her husband may or may not have died. She'd always been so good to me. Had I taken advantage of her kindness? I'd nearly stranded her as a widow with one son and another child on the way. Did she know how much I valued her?

The story of meeting Francie and the way she transformed my life never ceases to move me. We first met when I was living in an apartment in Sherman Oaks, finishing college. One of the ways I put myself through school was by renting an apartment bigger than what I needed and then taking in a roommate since half the rent of a two-bedroom apartment was less than the rent for one bedroom. My first roommate had moved out a few months earlier, and Brian Reilly, who our oldest son would eventually be named after, had moved in.

Brian's a great guy. He grew up in Long Island and graduated from SUNY on the East Coast before he landed with me in California. My place was on Sherman Way, which is a broad boulevard lined for miles with palm trees, and I had a little patio that overlooked the community pool. We'd grill chicken shish kebabs I made on a hibachi and drink Coors on that patio. Brian thought he'd died and gone to heaven. He loved the California lifestyle and wanted to live it to the max after decades in Long Island.

So this one day, I was hunched over my drafting table doing school work and he was down at the jacuzzi chatting up anyone he met, hanging with the babes. He met a young woman and came back to tell me about her. She had a roommate, he said.

"She was cute and nice. We should do something with them," he explained.

Later, Francie told me the story of how she'd ended up in that same apartment building. She'd just gotten back from traveling around Europe for a few months, a celebration of having completed nursing school before she started working the neonatal intensive care unit at UCLA. Her mom had offered her advice for picking out a place to live. "Well, honey, as you're checking out apartments, be sure to look at the pool area and see if there are guys there. See what the prospects look like." Francie just rolled her eyes. Little did she know that her mother's instincts would turn out to be spot-on.

That day Brian went to the jacuzzi, Francie's roommate, Sheila, had been hanging by the pool and he chatted her up. By the time he got back to our apartment, he had a plan.

"I know, Glen. We should have them over for dinner."

"Okay. We can do that. Why not? I'll make an invitation. What are their names?"

Brian hemmed and hawed. "I don't remember," he confessed. "But they live in apartment 353."

"How are we going to invite them to dinner if you don't remember their names? Besides, are *you* planning to cook?" By this point in our friendship, I'd yet to see Brian wield a skillet or figure out how to cook much of anything. I was doing it all.

"But you're so good at all that, Glen."

We decided we'd send them a formal invitation. I found a blank card and used my Leroy lettering set to make it look fancy, addressing the card, "To: Apartment 353. From: Apartment 267. You're cordially invited to a spaghetti dinner on the night of..."

I slipped it under their door and they soon RSVP'd. We were on.

Before they arrived, I tried to make the apartment look presentable. We didn't have a lot of stuff on the walls, so I got a bedsheet with a geometric repeating pattern, popular in the late seventies/early eighties, and pinned it on the corner of the wall. I must have seen this decorating hack somewhere and thought it was a good idea. It's amazing Francie stuck around after that. She wasn't overly impressed by the evening.

In fact, she told me later, the only reason she'd agreed to come was because a nurse she worked with at UCLA, Harriet, had urged her to go. After working twelve hours caring for sick newborns,

Francie was tired and just wanted to climb into bed, but Harriet bugged her. "You should go because you just never know…"

Years later, at the wedding, Harriet took full responsibility. If she hadn't bugged Francie, she told everyone, maybe we never would have met.

After her twelve-hour shift, Francie drove all the way back from UCLA and changed out of her nurse's uniform to join us. We'd planned the dinner late to accommodate her work schedule, and though she really just wanted to be in bed, she made an effort.

What I remember of that night were all my faux pas. For instance, I wore a suit. I'd just come from work but didn't take the time to change. Between the three-piece suit and knowing that I drove a newer BMW, Francie thought I was stuck up. The sheet thumbtacked to the wall didn't help. She was not at all engaged in the conversation that night, and I figured that was the end of it.

But soon Brian and I started hanging out with Sheila and Francie as a group, planning outings, going bowling, roller-blading, becoming a pack of friends. In time, she saw I wasn't stuck up and got over that initial impression. I was smitten with Francie but was also certain she was out of my league. So when Brian kind of paired off with Sheila, I figured maybe Francie and I could at least be friends.

All that changed, though, when Francie's family went on a river rafting trip and Brian and Sheila couldn't make it. Francie and I were driving up to Sacramento together, and her impression of me shifted. I still thought she was out of my league, but for the first time, she started to entertain the idea of us as a couple.

Hmmm, she thought. *This could have potential.*

Turns out, she'd prayed to meet someone back before that fateful spaghetti dinner night. She's always been a believer, and initially, we were very different in this way. She asked God to help her meet someone nice, who was kind and gentle, smart, hardworking with good morals, and who would be a good father. After she'd said

"Amen" to that prayer, the thought entered her mind to amend the prayer to ask for someone who was also tall; she loved tall men. But then she reconsidered. It seemed like a lot to request. Tall would be nice, but not necessary. As it turns out, I'm six feet four. As she sees it, God must've thought, *Because you didn't ask for tall, I'm going to give you tall in a big way!*

On that river rafting trip, another girl who wasn't part of our group approached Francie. "Hey, is that guy Glen your boyfriend?" This girl was apparently interested in me (little did I know!) and wanted to be sure I was in the clear before she made a move. In that instant, Francie had a sense of what was what and realized her prayer may have been answered.

"Yeah, he's my boyfriend," she told the girl. *Back off,* she thought.

Soon enough, though, I figured it out. We made a good pair and everyone around us, family and friends, saw that. One time, when we'd been dating only a little while, we decided to drive to Carmel to visit my grandparents. For me to drive Francie's little Datsun F-10, I needed to slide the driver's seat all the way back, which necessitated flipping the second seat up. When I went to do that as we were departing, Francie suddenly remembered a *Bride's* magazine she had purchased and left on the back seat.

"Don't put that seat back!" she commanded, not wanting me to see the magazine. I couldn't imagine why, but since it was important to her, I drove to Carmel with my knees against the steering wheel for five hours. Francie had figured out that I was *the one* but wanted to leave me time to figure out she was *the one* for me.

As is often the case, I am not as quick as Francie, but eventually I caught up with her. Ever since, I've known I am so much more with her at my side than I ever could be by myself.

By the time of the plane crash, we'd already bought our first house in Oceanside in northern San Diego County and had started our family with our firstborn, Brian. We were over the moon about the new baby who would join us soon.

But as Francie made her way frantically to the Huntington Beach Hospital, she worried that everything we'd been building was crashing down around us. Thankfully, that wasn't the case for us, though it was for the pilot, Dave. He'd been married only six months, and he died in that crash, his chest having smashed into the yoke, killing him upon impact. The others survived, many with injuries. I suffered only a hairline fracture. How was that possible?

I'D LEARNED AN IMPORTANT LESSON ABOUT MY FAMILY. YES, I NEEDED TO GO OUT OF MY WAY TO INVEST IN MYSELF, BUT EVEN MORE SO IN THEM.

Sometime after that crash, the insurance people took me to the plane so I could see it. They asked if I wanted to take anything from the wreck. I chose the altimeter, and to this day, I keep it on my desk. Whenever I thought I was having a hard day, that altimeter, set at the elevation of Meadowlark Airport, gave me perspective.

I'd learned an important lesson about my family. Yes, I needed to go out of my way to invest in myself, but even more so in them.

When I was nineteen, I received a personal handwritten thank-you note from a printer for my insignificant $13 order of business cards. When I held the card in my hand and thought of the person who'd taken the time and effort to write it, I felt important. That card made me feel as if I and my business mattered. It was such a small thing, but it had a profound effect on me. I decided then and there that henceforth I'd write personal notes as often as possible to work colleagues, friends, clients, anyone I could think of to tell them they mattered to me. I did and I continue to do so. As a result, I can now trace lifelong friendships and millions of dollars to those handwritten notes.

I carried that attitude, and expanded it, to my relationship with Francie. Though I credit the fact we're still married to her tenacious stubbornness—no way was she going to give up on us—I have also tried to do my part by paying attention. In other word, as I've already touched on, Francie regularly receives handwritten notes.

I soon realized that everyone likes and needs different things, and so you have to pay attention to find out what's important to another person. For instance, we celebrate our anniversary not only on the twenty-sixth of June but on the twenty-sixth of *each* month. We dub it Anniversary Date Night and do something special.

I've come up with other, fun, creative ways to make memories. For instance, back in the nineties, it seemed every week brought a new Victoria's Secret catalog in the mail. One featured the Fantasy Bra, custom-made with diamonds all over it, costing more than a million dollars. To surprise Francie, I decided to make her one of her own. I went to the Victoria's Secret store at the local mall to buy a plain bra as close in structure as I could find to the custom one. Then I got a bunch of rhinestones and fake crystals that I applied with glue. She loved it.

Recently, I made sure our bathroom was "featured" on the cover of *Bend Home and Style*. Another year, on Valentine's Day, I presented her with an official notice from the State Board of Holidays, informing her that the holiday would be celebrated, that year only, on March 9. That date change allowed me to surprise her with a trip.

Yet another year, I made sure she received an important communique from the Department of Homeland Security, warning her of a credible threat that a "Hopeless Romantic" terrorist had plans to kidnap her. "While he may take you hostage, we believe that a release can eventually be negotiated, so we recommend you do not try to escape." The letter warned that he planned to take her to his hideout on the coast, exact location unknown, and that she should pack a small overnight bag with needed essentials. "Keep in mind you are dealing with a fanatic [fanatically in love with you], and he may be prone to irrational outbursts [of love]. It's important for your safety and survival that you play along until the authorities can rescue you."

Just like it takes forethought and planning to make a successful backpacking trip, personal growth and relationships with others don't just happen by accident. They're something you invest in. When you have space in your life to "do more," then you are free to do the things that add depth, joy, and meaning to your life. For me, depth, joy, and meaning are almost always connected with people. I've found that I need to invest time and energy into those relationships to reap the rewards and to make the lives of those I care about rewarding for them.

LESSON 9

Use a Compass

A FEW MONTHS AFTER THAT FATAL PLANE CRASH, I WAS STILL periodically having nightmares of aviation smashups on a regular basis. But my sleep was dreamless the night Francie woke me with her urgent words.

"I'm in labor," she said.

As we pulled out of the driveway, our neighbor Lisa dashed across the street in the dark to watch over sleeping Brian until our friend Tammy could get there, as we prepared to welcome our second child.

Francie and I had long discussed the size of the ideal family. Because there had been three of us kids in my family growing up, I thought three was the perfect number. Francie, though, came from a family of four and thus was convinced four was perfect. Either way, we were both excited to be adding to our family with birth number two. Because it was 1987 and ultrasounds were not commonly used unless there was a reason for concern, we didn't know the baby's gender, size, or much about him or her. We couldn't wait to see our child's beautiful face, to finally touch the elbows and knees that had been protruding from Francie's belly for some time now.

We'd agreed, back before we were married, to raise our children Catholic since Francie was Catholic and I didn't have any belief in

God or a specific transcendent power. I hadn't grown up with any formal religious training, but my mother had joined the Quakers (Society of Friends) when we moved back East after the divorce, and we all went to Quaker meeting as a family. As I became a teen, Mom gave us kids the option at some point to attend or not. While I'd gotten something out of the quiet, meditative gatherings and the sometimes profound insights that were shared in the meeting house, when given the choice, I decided to enjoy my Sunday mornings in other pursuits. I had long strived to live an upright, moral life, but the idea of a God who intervened in human affairs and who was personal to me, that just didn't make sense. Maybe I was too much of an engineer, too analytic. I lived and worked in the physical world and was used to the scientific method of a hypothesis based on observations, then testing that hypothesis with appropriate experiments.

During the process of preparing for marriage, Francie and I attended an Engaged Encounter weekend. The workshop was presented under the aegis of the Roman Catholic Church but was focused on having a successful marriage, not on questions of personal faith. At our premarital meeting with the priest who would marry us, I had to agree that I understood that Francie had an obligation to bring up any children we might have in the Catholic faith. There was no requirement at the time that I become Catholic. Francie mentioned years later that she had been concerned about marrying someone who didn't share her faith and beliefs, but she figured that since the priest didn't seem concerned, she figured it would work out somehow.

It was years later that I decided to attend some RCIA (Rite of Christian Initiation for Adults) classes at St. Patrick's, one of our local Catholic churches, in an effort to gain a window into Francie's faith. I had been attending Mass with Francie since we started dating, so I knew the general outline. I was looking forward to learning more about the specifics of the Catholic faith, to see if I could join Francie and the kids and share their religion. The first couple of classes mostly covered things about the church that I had pretty much picked up on my own. When I arrived for the third class, there was a sign-up sheet, but before I could attend that class, I was told, "To learn the rest, you need to become a Catholic." That didn't make sense to me. How was I to decide if I wanted to join if I didn't know what was involved? While I was interested in learning more, I didn't feel I had absorbed enough at that stage to commit to becoming Catholic. I took my commitments seriously and was not interested in committing to something about which I wasn't sufficiently informed. So I turned around and walked out.

Still, someone had said something to me after the plane crash that had stuck with me—that "God had a plan for my life." Was that true, and if so, what was that plan? It was clear that Francie drew deep comfort and purpose from her faith. And while I would have liked to have something just as comforting, for reasons I didn't understand, I couldn't figure out how to take hold of that kind of faith.

That all changed with the birth of our second child in 1987.

When the baby didn't progress through the birth canal as anticipated, the doctor opted for a cesarean section. The minute we saw Derek—another boy!—we had just the slightest inkling that things would be different this time around. His head was maybe a little larger than we expected, but he was beautiful! Soon enough, though, I learned harsh terms I would have been okay with never knowing.

Derek was born with hydrocephalus, a condition involving an accumulation of cerebrospinal fluid in the brain, which causes increased pressure within the skull. This condition can occur before birth or later in life. One to two newborns per thousand are born hydrocephalic. When hydrocephalus occurs in utero, as it had with Derek, the additional pressure in the skull prevents the brain from growing and developing normally. Doctors are not sure of the causes of hydrocephalus in newborns. Because of her medical background and experience in neonatal intensive care units, Francie had a pretty good idea of what we were dealing with, though I was mostly in the dark. Derek would suffer from constant seizure activity, blindness, severe mental retardation, poor muscle tone and coordination, hyper gag reflex, cerebral palsy... the list went on and on. He needed constant and complete care for all his needs. I didn't know how we were going to deal with the additional burdens this placed on us.

Caring for him became a full-time job, and it fell almost entirely on Francie. Derek required four bottles a day to gain strength, but it took two hours to feed him a bottle. Because he had a hyper-sensitive gag reflex, he'd often gag and throw up most of the last bottle, and the whole process would have to start again. Hydrocephalus is typically treated with a surgically placed shunt to drain the excess spinal fluid. Derek had six surgeries in his first twelve months of life trying to get his shunt to work. Each surgery was an entire ordeal of doctor's visits, consultations with specialists, hospital stays, and recovery periods.

I was busy working all the time—seventy or eighty hours a week—to keep our family solvent. I had just started my first firm, Pacific Rim Engineering, and our company's monthly health premiums went from $600 to more than $8,000 within six months of his birth. This need to provide also gave me an excuse, I realized later, to hide out at work and not face this heartbreak head-on. Francie was left to handle all of this, in addition to caring for two-year-old Brian. She worried constantly: Had she done something wrong during the pregnancy? Was Derek's condition somehow her fault?

I held Derek many times, and in general he was a happy kid. He responded to music, maybe more so because of his inability to see. He responded to motion and loved to be spun around in his stroller and, later, his wheelchair. He was ticklish and would start laughing when I rubbed his chest. Sometimes, he would just be lying there by himself, and he would suddenly smile, then start a screaming joyous laugh, and would laugh so hard he would start choking, then recover, then start all over again. We used to speculate that angels were tickling him or whispering jokes in his ears.

Other times, Derek cried and screamed incessantly, and Francie did all she could to comfort him, but she was reaching the end of her rope. She is the toughest woman I know. It takes a lot to put her under; most other women would have tapped out long before Francie. Besides Derek, she cared for her harried husband, an active toddler, and then, with the arrival of our third son, Grant, a second newborn. It is beyond humbling, after your own strength is long gone, to watch the woman you love give the last drop of her strength caring for your child, a child who would never send her cards, never say thank you, never tell her he loved her—and I'm talking about *before* he became a teenager. She hung on and hung in there, but the whole time, her heart was breaking, and I was usually absent, at the office all the time.

I could see the strain it was taking on Francie, but I didn't know what to do to help. That's when I started to open myself up to the idea of faith and God. My whole life, I'd been confronted with problems, most of which I could solve with my intellect and hard work. And those I couldn't solve, I could ameliorate, improve the conditions, make things better. But this? Wow. It was so far beyond me and my skill set. I had never been stumped this badly before. And it hurt in my heart whenever I thought of Derek and the pain Francie was experiencing caring for him. I was frustrated and numb.

Not knowing where you are or where you are heading can be an overwhelming experience. On a backpacking trip in the wilderness, it can be dangerous. On a 2009 hike in the Wind Rivers Range in western Wyoming with Wilderness Trekking School led by Andrew Skurka, I got lost.

Skurka, besides his incredible skills for analysis and his amazing strength and endurance, has an almost supernatural ability to know where he is on the landscape. As a civil engineer, I'm comfortable with topographic maps and generally have a decent sense of direction. But on this trip, the group had become separated, and Skurka had run ahead while I was to accompany the group to the planned campsite. I felt something was off. The trail didn't seem quite as it was described, but we forged on.

IN THE END WE DECIDED TO RETRACE OUR STEPS. SOMETIMES GOING BACKWARD IS THE FASTEST WAY TO REACH YOUR DESTINATION.

We tried taking some bearings off of mountains to triangulate, but there were a *lot* of mountains around, and it was hard to distinguish between them. We thought we knew the direction we were going, but then we came to a lake that wasn't on the map, at least not where we thought we were. We had to admit we were lost. We could not get oriented and did not know which direction we should take.

In the end we decided to retrace our steps. Sometimes going backward is the fastest way to reach your destination. Sure enough, Skurka found us and guided us to the correct location. In the wilderness, as in life, to get to where you want to go, you first have to know where you are, and in life at least, who you are. This is where using a compass or having someone who knows the terrain better than you do can be a life changer. Admitting that you are lost can be the first step in getting the right kind of help.

During our crisis with taking care of Derek, I felt lost. I did not know where we were heading; this was uncharted territory for us. I was overwhelmed and did not know what to do. In desperation, I thought, *What if there is a power greater than me that I could lean on?* Intuitively, I felt that God could offer some relief from the pain I was experiencing and maybe provide a way of making sense of things. While faith didn't make everything perfect for Francie, it was a source of deep strength for her. Maybe I could use my engineer's mind (I know, trouble!) to figure out this God thing.

By this time, though Brian still attended a Catholic school, together we'd started attending a small evangelical church with friends of ours; I enjoyed going there and listening to the sermons. I had always been curious about spiritual things. That's why I'd been in the plane when it crashed; I was trying to understand better my role in life, how I could improve. Before settling on this new church home, Francie had sent me to explore a few other churches, and now we felt we were where we belonged. Every morning, I spent some time reading the Psalms in the Bible, reaching for the comfort she found there, but I didn't feel anything. How was this all supposed to work if I didn't believe in God? I didn't know how to take the next step.

It was a Saturday afternoon, and I was dealing with lawn care. You can have your life breaking into pieces around you, but the lawn still has to be mowed. I'd been vexed for the past month by a gopher ripping up our backyard. That, at least, was a problem I should be able to fix. But I hadn't been able to. I'd tried everything to get rid of the tunneling rodent, from putting smoke bombs into the tunnels to filling up the holes. Nothing was working. What started as one small hole had now blossomed into what looked like an entire colony. I finally decided I'd just have to flush them out, *Caddyshack* style.

Our backyard was a little bit higher than the front of the house, and there was a little gopher hole near the right-hand side in front as you looked up at the garage. That was the lowest point and where a gopher would likely appear if my flood-'em-out plan succeeded. I put a hose into one of the upper gopher holes, turned the faucet on, and waited. Nothing. No sign of a gopher anywhere.

Okay, then, it was time for the big guns. I turned the water pressure on harder, full bore now. Gallons of water were spurting full blast into the earth, but nothing was happening. The water had to come out somewhere! Soon, a little trickle started to flow at that low point by the front of the garage. I took a shovel and waited. My only chance of success was if the gopher showed up at this exit.

While I waited, I prayed. It's not like I'd set out this day to test God, but suddenly, the words were in my mouth.

"Okay, God, I get the whole eternal salvation thing. I'm on board. And I accept that maybe Derek is the way he is because of some reason I don't understand, that he has a power and a purpose in this world that has not been revealed to me, and that if I could see him from your all-loving perspective, I could accept the hardships. But what I need to know is, Are you any good for the day-to-day stuff? Like this stupid gopher who is making a mess of my yard?"

Just as I finished my prayer, a gopher started sputtering up out of that hole. I whacked him with the shovel, and in that moment, I felt for the first time that this mysterious idea of a God who might be personal to me and might care about my life was real. God had answered my prayer, saying, *Okay, if you need a gopher to believe, then here's a gopher.* Funny, I never again had an issue with gophers in the yard. After dispatching the gopher and turning off the hose, I walked around the corner to our neighbors Glenn and Judy, who were fervent believers, and said, "What must I do to be saved?"

I'd always been a chronic worrier—I had even developed an ulcer in middle school with my apprehensions and concerns. But after that day, I felt relief, having encountered an all-loving God who I could just hand those worries over to.

That day is what I now like to call my "gopher conversion." I know it sounds silly, but it was what I needed. Thankfully, over time, and in many ways due to Derek, my relationship with God through his Son, Jesus, grew and matured. I understand now that God is not here to solve my gopher problems. But from that experience, I saw that day that he was interested in my individual struggle because he cared for me. He may or may not solve the problems I bring to him, but he is always there *with* me in the problems. He provides a compass that orients me, letting me know where I am headed and, sometimes more importantly, letting me know when I have strayed and gotten lost.

Sometimes he directs me toward someone else who may help me solve my issue. Or better still, maybe he sends someone *my* way so I can help them solve *their* concern. God often works, I have come to see, through the hands of others. And he relies on my hands to do a portion of that work.

I do believe in the God as revealed in the Bible and believe that everyone needs a personal relationship with God through his Son, Jesus Christ. But I understand that people have their own opinions and beliefs. In most cases, they are unlikely to change their minds based on my beliefs. But if they want to know about Jesus, I'll tell them what I know. Mostly, I'm just humbled by what I've experienced. My faith teaches me that I am to follow the example of Jesus whenever possible, becoming more like him every day. The more time I spend getting to know Jesus, the more I know I still have a long way to go. I also feel a kind of confidence that had previously been missing in my life. If, as I believe, we are all adopted, through Jesus, as sons and daughters of the Most High God, then we are all royalty and need to treat each other as such.

This means that I'm responsible to help those I can. In order to do so, I'm given grace to walk through the challenges life poses. This knowledge, at last, gave me the peace I'd long wanted. Even as a kid I'd worried myself sick, thinking I needed to be responsible for my mother and siblings after the divorce, that I needed to be more than I was. Now, I could let go of those expectations and allow myself to be human and flawed, unable to fix a lot of things but also confident that the God of my understanding would take care of those elements I could not myself repair.

And so, though I've become a believer, that doesn't mean that God speaks to me directly or that I have any special insight into how life is supposed to work, apart from the Holy Spirit revealing things to me in Scripture or prayer.

There's been only one time that God spoke to me directly. I was at my wit's end after Derek's birth, crying, distraught, and almost certain I was going to lose Francie to the depression that was swamping her. I needed her, and the thought that she might break irreparably scared the daylights out of me.

I got angry at God. *Do you even exist? If so, how could you let this happen?!* My chest felt like it was encased in steel bands. *Do you even care?*

This was the one and only time God spoke to me, but his words were clear as a bell.

"Francie will get better," God said. "And that will be my sign to you."

Things got worse before they got better, and it was a very long road that we are still traveling. But she *did* get better, and I never doubted seriously again.

Still, as a result of Francie's severe clinical depression, we realized the pressure of caring for Derek was becoming too much for her to bear. By then, I was still working far too many hours and Francie was mostly alone, caring for Brian, who was five, and our newborn, Grant, as well as Derek, who at two and a half was in a crib or a stroller and couldn't feed himself, couldn't crawl, could not even sit up. Derek had endless appointments for occupational and physical therapy. Francie would have two babies crying at 4:00 a.m., one breastfeeding and one who couldn't hold his own bottle. It was simply too much, and she realized it.

Her father came and we searched out care arrangements for Derek. Hour upon hour, Francie's father, Lou, sat in bureaucrats' offices trying to get the approval needed to place Derek in a homecare facility. He was told the particular bureaucrat he needed to meet with wasn't available, even after Lou had sent countless letters trying to arrange an appointment.

THIS MEANS THAT I'M RESPONSIBLE TO HELP THOSE I CAN. IN ORDER TO DO SO, I'M GIVEN GRACE TO WALK THROUGH THE CHALLENGES LIFE POSES.

"That's okay. I'll wait for him," Lou said to the secretary.

"No, you should go home. We don't know when he'll be back."

"That's okay. I'll still wait. I'm not leaving until I have the approval letter in my hands."

Lou was persistent and tenacious, trying to arrange the best possible situation for Derek. Once we got approval for him to be placed, Lou and Francie looked at a number of facilities. Some of the places were heartbreaking—they were so poorly run, you wouldn't leave your dog there. They smelled terrible, or you could see that the residents were not well cared for. Finally, we found a state institution in Costa Mesa geared toward kids, and Derek was accepted.

He moved into Fairview Developmental Center and was now about an hour away from us. He got great care there, and the staff doted on him. Fairview was built next to the Costa Mesa golf course, right next to Newport Beach. We used to joke that our son Derek lived in a high rise in Newport Beach, surrounded by a golf course, and was into music.

We visited periodically as a family, bringing his brothers along. It was important to us that the brothers knew each other. Francie visited all the time, much more than the rest of us. She decorated his rooms, prayed over him, and took him special audio tapes, hand-made quilts, and new clothes. She built relationships with his care-givers, other Fairview clients, and their parents. To whatever extent Derek could know anything, he knew he was loved.

I believe that for Brian and Grant, the experience growing up with a brother who was severely disabled and in a wheelchair gave them more tender hearts. They don't fear people in wheelchairs, as some folks do, and they have greater compassion for what's involved, for the frailties of the human condition. They made sacrifices growing up because of Derek, and they never complained. I know the experience of raising Derek changed both me and Francie deeply. Francie has touched many other parents of disabled kids, able to render comfort and compassion because she has walked the road they are traveling. It's a journey you can't understand until you find yourself on it.

Derek lived until he was almost twenty. Since he was confined to a bed, he was always prone to respiratory issues. He got pneumonia for the umpteenth time and ended up in the local Orange County hospital, where he was put on a ventilator. He gradually improved and was eventually taken off that ventilator with a tracheotomy. Then Derek suffered a cardiac arrest and was put on life support. We had to make the hardest, most agonizing decision of our life, to remove life support.

On Mother's Day that year, Derek finally went to be with Jesus.

There is no happy ending to this story unless you look at it through the lens of faith. Because of Derek's condition and the fact that I ran headlong into a problem I could not in a million years fix, I was given the grace to see that there were greater forces at work. I realized a higher power exists, and I needed that power to see me through. Would I have found this faith if not for Derek's presence in my life? I don't know. I'm only glad that I have it now.

And so while I'm not someone who goes around trying to evangelize others, I do share how my life became simpler, more straightforward, and more fulfilling since I found my way to faith.

I realize that people believe all kinds of different things and may not change those beliefs based on my testimony. But I will say this: when life hits you hard, as it did to me with Derek's illness and eventual death, a tragedy in which I also feared I might lose my wife because her grief was so very deep, it's essential to believe in something greater, stronger, and more powerful than yourself. Being out on the trail, dwarfed by towering cliffs or enormous trees, standing in awe at wildlife or a stunning sunset, I marvel that the Creator of this infinitely incredible world knows and cares for me, providing me a spiritual compass to live by. Being in the majesty of the wilderness reminds me of how small I am.

LESSON 10

Practice Generosity

"But Glen, I don't know how to sew, and I don't know anyone who can sew."

I heard this sentence again and again, the words uttered by some person who had discovered my pack design on the early internet but couldn't figure out how to end up with one of their own.

A few handy souls rose to the occasion and fashioned packs of their own, and it's a treat when I'm speaking at an event and someone brings their handmade, typically well-used pack to show me. But most, especially men whose mothers hadn't made sure they knew how to sew before they left home—thanks, Mom!—were utterly stumped. While they were intrigued by the lightweight pack I'd devised, even with my far-too-detailed instructions, they couldn't figure out how to make one or how to have one made.

I dubbed that first pack the "G1." It had been based very loosely on the Alpine Rucksack mentioned in Jardine's book. Every time I hiked with the pack, I thought of ways I could improve it. This led to various iterations, including the one that shredded itself to nothing in Brian's hands on a Sierra trek, until I settled on what I perceived to be the perfect lightweight pack for me at that point, the G4. (Nobody ever accused me of being overly creative when it came to names.)

To help people who wanted to make their own, I wrote up the instructions with dimensioned pattern pieces and put them online, free for the taking. I figured it was the least I could do. I was just then embracing one of the mottoes that would come to steer my life, to give freely to others whenever possible, and it felt good to give away what had taken me countless hours to create, knowing my efforts would benefit others.

Because my life was unencumbered by unnecessary stuff, I was able to do more. That does not mean I should "make more." I had the freedom to follow our deep instinct to do good in the world, and so my first impulse was to give away freely what I could to others.

Still, though, the calls, requests, and emails kept coming. *Could you sew one for me? Please?*

It was just not possible. The process took about ten hours for one pack, from marking the fabric to cutting it to sewing it all together. I was working full time as a civil engineer, so unless the person wanted to pay me a king's ransom for such a pack, it made no sense. I had no time to spare, and the packs, if I were to sew them myself, would be far too expensive for anyone to afford. I kept redirecting these requests to the website where they could download the pattern. Hopefully they could find someone who knew how to sew.

Still, the requests kept coming, and I felt bad. I wanted others to experience the freedom I'd found with the lighter pack. Being more lightweight on the trail had transformed backpacking for me and Read Miller. I would come back from hikes to a few more emails asking about how to get ahold of a G4 pack. Even when Read and I hiked, we'd run into folks who'd heard of my designs.

"I'd really love one of those packs. Can you make one for me?"

I set about seeing if there was a way to make a few to quell the pleas.

First, I asked Francie if she might sew a few for me. She's a master seamstress, and my pattern wasn't all that demanding. Keep in mind, though, that I'm an engineer. And though I know my way around a sewing machine and have a strong grasp of design principles, I am not formally trained in sewing techniques. I gave Francie my pattern and directions and left her to it. I thought what I'd concocted was straightforward, but she kept coming back to me with questions.

"Does this need to be lined up with the grain?" she asked.

I didn't know.

"What do these marks here indicate?"

I showed her.

"Does this need to line up with the seam?"

It soon became clear that we spoke different languages when sewing, mine rooted in engineering lingo. She made a few packs for me but grumbled throughout about the poor pattern design and the instructions I'd provided. Eventually, I decided that with all the feedback I had to give her, it would be just as easy for me to make them myself. Since I hadn't come from the sewing world as she had, my pattern read more like an architectural blueprint than a real pattern.

Soon, though, Francie was able to translate my design into a pattern she could better follow, and together with a neighbor who was also a seamstress, they made a few for me. Still, the value of the hours required to construct such a pack went far beyond what I might reasonably charge. That was okay, though. I wasn't trying to make money, just helping out some folks.

It's long been part of my makeup to give away what I can to others. I think fondly of the couple back in Iowa who made us breakfast on

the cross-country bike trek and how their generosity touched me. Sure, it took some effort to draw up the design plans for the pack, but what I'd done to benefit my own life could now help others. And making a few packs and coordinating with Francie and our neighbor for a few more was little skin off my nose. Meanwhile, those receiving the packs were overjoyed with them, sharing their stories with me, filling my heart. It was a fair trade-off.

I NAMED THIS FLEDGLING BUSINESS GVP GEAR AND FIGURED THAT ONCE I HAD THOSE TWENTY-FIVE PACKS, I WOULD BE DONE AND COULD GET ON WITH MY LIFE.

So though Francie and our neighbor had by this time made a few packs for people, just trying to be good hiking citizens in the backcountry world, it was clear that wasn't going to be a solution for the continued requests we were getting.

I was having a conversation with one of the sisters at Quest Outfitters in Florida, where I got my fabrics and hardware, and I explained my dilemma.

"I saw an ad in an industry magazine for a cut-and-sew operation up in Seattle," she suggested. "Maybe try them."

Seattle was at least on the same coast. Perfect! I called them up and was introduced to Monty. I told him I wanted him to make twenty-five packs for me. I figured that would take care of everyone who wanted one, and I could get back to my engineering. Not having much time to think about it, I named this fledgling business GVP Gear and figured that once I had those twenty-five packs, I would be done and could get on with my life.

"Oh." The manufacturer was stumped by my request. "Our minimum order is a hundred."

One hundred! That was crazy. I could not imagine one hundred people being interested in owning a G4 pack. I explained this, and we talked around it for a while, eventually compromising on an order of fifty. I assumed I'd have packs in my garage for the next five years, but I'd eventually find people who could use them.

I sent Monty my pattern, the fabric needed to make a sample, and a pack I had sewn. He was used to making packs for major companies, and I thought he'd immediately catch on to what I was doing. Not so. He was initially confused by my pack design. After a series of exchanges, going back and forth, with me explaining how and why each pack they attempted was still not right, the manufacturer realized we were doing something quite different.

"These are not like other packs we've made," Monty said.

Exactly! That was the whole point. To do something that no one else had done, something way lighter yet more functional. Finally, we had a good working model and were ready to roll. I ordered enough fabric for fifty packs.

I had no idea what was coming.

The internet at this time was gaining steam, and Brian put together an early website for me. People could go to that site, fill in a form, and choose the color of pack they wanted: red, black, royal blue, or green (and a second choice on color if applicable). Almost no one picked the green. The size was what fit me at six feet four. Looking back, I think it's crazy that I didn't offer different sizes for short or average folks, but I clearly thought color selection was an important consideration. (For the next twenty years, we would offer almost no color choices because I eventually realized how needlessly complicated extra colors makes things.)

Whenever an order came in, I wrote it down on a yellow legal pad, and we shipped the packs out.

The G4 is basically a large tube that poofs out at the bottom for a sleeping bag, with huge mesh side pockets. The shoulder straps get filled out with sleeping socks added by the backpacker. A Z-rest sectioned pad provides the frame. The roll top fastens to the sides with hook and loop. The pack itself, despite having a capacity of over 50 liters, weighs under a pound. Very simple and practical.

Word spread quickly on the internet, and the G4s stacked in my garage didn't stay there long. Soon I was placing orders for a hundred at a time with Monty, filling my garage to capacity with backpacks. My sister Brooke put together a new more robust website to handle the orders.

As I corresponded with customers, if I found out they needed their packs for the Pacific Crest Trail, I would often invite them to stay with Francie and me as they prepared to start their trek. There's a long tradition of Trail Angels helping those who are thru-hikers—offering food to supplement a hiker's stash, maybe a warm meal, a hot shower, perhaps a haircut, or a couch to sleep on for a night, away from the trail. Some Trail Angels, like Barney and Sandy Mann in San Diego and Donna and Jeff Saufley of Agua Dulce, have created highly developed juggernaut systems to attend to hikers. In our own more humble version, we met people flying in from, say, England or Minnesota or wherever they were coming from, ready to start on what would typically be five months on the trail. After picking them up at the airport, we hosted them in our Carlsbad home as they acquired last-minute items, did gear shakedowns, and mailed resupply packages ahead. Then we drove them to the Mexican border to start.

Many nights when the kids were younger, we'd have a house full with hikers sleeping all over the living room and some in tents on the back lawn. My instinct to do this was not just because of the Trail Angel idea but because that's how I'd grown up. My mom often had people staying with us—usually artists rather than hikers, but the same idea held. When people might benefit from sharing some of what I have, it's incumbent on me to make the free offer if I can.

GVP Gear just kept growing. I was doing what I set out to do, sharing with others the design I'd created that would simplify their outings, only now the business was eating up more and more of my time. I was still working long hours as a civil engineer, but now my nights and weekends were spent emailing customers and suppliers and shipping backpacks. I wasn't taking a salary or any income from this endeavor, and it was consuming an increasing chunk of my life. This wasn't what I intended.

In order to free me up a bit, I realized I'd need to make some changes. One option was to raise the prices so I could hire someone to oversee the business, but I really didn't want to do that. The packs originally sold for $70, and that included priority mail postage! Backpackers, in the aggregate, tend to be people who place more emphasis on experiences than making money. I didn't want those, like my future colleague Rilee at Sparrow Bakery, to be priced out of an innovation that would help them.

Then it hit me: if I offered more products and created a kind of synergy with the company's offerings, that might generate enough volume to allow for some efficiencies of scale. I started making lightweight trekking poles in the garage and carrying other merchandise, soon developing lightweight tarps that would pair with the trekking poles for an integrated shelter system. And the orders kept coming in.

At one point, the website Backpacking Light, in an effort to make more cottage gear available to the burgeoning swell of ultralight customers, created a fulfillment system. They put up a website for small gear manufacturers like me and would handle all the orders and shipping. Perfect!

I drove from Carlsbad to Bozeman, Montana, to deliver my merchandise to Backpacking Light. Finally, I could concentrate again on our family—the boys were getting older—as well as my own hiking adventures, my career, and spending time with my adorable wife.

We likely would have chugged on that way had Francie not come home one day and seen the bill I was paying for the order fulfillment. The fee was based on a sliding scale, depending on order volume. As the volume of our orders had grown, so had the size of the monthly checks I was writing to Backpacking Light.

"For that kind of money, I could do it myself!"

Seriously? You want to do that? Okay, then. Your wish is my command.

I rented a van and drove all the merchandise back to Carlsbad from Bozeman, and Francie became the head of shipping. By this time, GVP Gear had become an official company with a new name, Gossamer Gear, playing off the G initial I loved so much. Our tagline at the time was "Innovative. Ultralight. Affordable."

The years passed and the business showed nice steady growth, though I didn't pay it too much attention. As I said earlier, I had only started the company to give to others a way of backpacking that had greatly enriched my life. I wasn't doing it to get rich, and I still wasn't taking a salary. I was paid handsomely, though, just by seeing others converted to what some jokingly called "the way of Glen."

I joined the Pacific Crest Trail Association (PCTA) board of directors as another way to give back to the community that had augmented my life. I also gave talks wherever and whenever asked, teaching others techniques and hacks for lightening one's load.

"What about John Mackey?" asked Henry Shires, founder of Tarptent and a fellow PCTA board member, at a breakout session of a board meeting weekend in Seattle. We were discussing people who might join the board as members when the terms of current members expired. "I hear he's a big hiker. He might like to join us."

"Who's that?" I asked.

"Cofounder of Whole Foods Market. We should ask him."

"Anyone have contact info?"

Liz Bergeron, our executive director, got in touch with Mackey and set up a dinner for the two of us to meet with him when he was in Boulder. I was going to be there anyway to speak at a Continental Divide Trail Alliance event, so it worked for me.

I HAD ONLY STARTED THE COMPANY TO GIVE TO OTHERS A WAY OF BACKPACKING THAT HAD GREATLY ENRICHED MY LIFE. I WASN'T DOING IT TO GET RICH.

When I got home from the board meeting, I checked my yellow legal pad. Turns out, Mackey had ordered a fair amount of gear from Gossamer Gear; I just hadn't recognized the name because I didn't shop at Whole Foods.

A few weeks later, I flew to Denver and got up to Boulder to meet Mackey at a local vegan restaurant. Liz and I had a nice dinner with John. We talked a lot about hiking and gear and also about the important work that the PCTA was doing. After the meeting, Liz went back to Sacramento, and after my talk, I headed back to Carlsbad.

I was still working more than full time at my "real" job and volunteering where I could. And though Gossamer Gear had been my baby, it was one I could no longer carve out sufficient time to care for. Even with Francie handling the shipping, it was still eating too much into my free time and starting to encroach on my work hours as well. Since it had never paid me a salary, if one of my two jobs had to go, it would have to be Gossamer.

After some painstaking soul searching, and seeking the counsel of wise friends, I knew that shuttering the business was the only reasonable choice. I was saddened but also relieved.

Before I could put the decision into motion, though, the phone rang. It was Liz Bergeron.

"It's been a couple of weeks since we had dinner with John and proposed that he consider joining the board. You were the one with the connection, so you should do the follow-up."

I promptly called John and, after some small talk, asked if he had come to a decision about joining the PCTA board. He said he would not join the board but he would make a donation—which ended up, at the time, being the largest single-donor contribution to the PCTA.

As we were closing the conversation, I added an aside.

"I've decided to close Gossamer Gear. I'm working sixty hours a week doing engineering and thirty hours a week on Gossamer Gear, and it's just not sustainable. So if you want to buy any more gear, you should do it in the next week or two."

"I'm leaving on a hike," Mackey said, "but don't do anything until I get back. I'll give you a call."

What did that even mean? I had no idea.

When he later phoned me back, he launched right in.

"Gossamer Gear makes great products the world needs, Glen. For selfish reasons, I don't want to see it close down."

He had a business proposition waiting for me. "I propose to buy seventy-five percent of the company and invest additional funds to hire staff and build the enterprise. I already have someone willing to run it, a guy I thru-hiked with on the Appalachian Trail. You can be as involved or uninvolved as you choose. And you will keep 25 percent regardless of your involvement. Would that work for you?"

Would that work for me? I didn't see any downside, so I said, "Yes."

That would solve the problems that had long plagued me. Who would have guessed?

But the lesson here, for me, was realizing that this arrangement came about only because, at every juncture, I'd been invested in giving freely to the community that had long enriched me. I wasn't out to make a buck or to corner a market. What I've found is that, when I give freely of my resources, my talent, and my time, I am always rewarded. Sometimes that reward comes in beautiful sunsets over the ocean shared with friends, or sunrises at a campsite in the middle of the desert. Sometimes it's financial, and other times it's to be found in the precious richness of relationships and experiences. But when I give without restraint, I am more than compensated in one way or another.

In that spirit, I still have those original G4 instructions available for download at my website (see appendix). Maybe you'll be better at sewing than most.

Learn from Failure

"DOING MORE" SHOULD NOT BE EQUATED WITH FINDING MORE success. As an engineer and tinkerer, I'm always looking at things and thinking about a better way to do them. Sometimes this leads to an invention, a widget to accomplish some task or save time or weight. Or sometimes it's a process that could be improved, like my penchant for writing personal notes to let people know how much I appreciate them or their business or particular ways of running a company. A lot of times, I find myself thinking, *I can find a better way to do this*. Still, most of those efforts necessitate that there will be many failures along the way. I have discovered that it is best to befriend these failures and learn from them. In other words, if you're not failing, you're not trying hard enough.

When the kids were small, I started my own civil engineering firm. But when the California economy and its entire housing/building market tanked in 1993, I faced failure on an epic scale and learned more during that period of so-called failure than I would have had I encountered only continued success. I learned, first of all, that it's important to always have a cushion.

I realize that many people work paycheck to paycheck, and this can sound like privilege talking, but it's clear to me that giving oneself some kind of cushion, whenever and wherever possible, is vital. Even a small cushion can help. If we learn to live below our means, even a little below, there's some hope of surviving crushing defeats. When I live below my means—*take less!*—I'm more agile in responding to the inevitable hiccups that can seriously derail a life. This is true in the backcountry too. If I'm carrying a light load, my strength is available to help someone else who may be struggling.

Still, no matter how much of a margin I created, the economy cratering in such a huge way could not be offset by my planning. I was tempted to take the setback personally. I had built a strong and well-thought-out business and yet, due to factors beyond my control, that business was now faltering. Because I'd long stressed the importance of living below our means in our family, I was able to work for a year without taking a salary and took out a second mortgage on our family's home to keep the business going.

Still, the factors lined up against us were greater than all my resourcefulness and preparation. Even the best planning in the world can be for naught when other circumstances intervene. Eventually, after making sure all my employees found other jobs, I had to shutter that business. I felt deep sadness in doing so, and yet I didn't let that so-called failure define me.

I have found that success often comes out of many failures. In some of my failures, I have come face-to-face with the fact I just don't know enough to do what I'm trying to do. There's no shame in that. I still have worth and value, despite what I don't know. Also, an amazing thing happens when I admit I don't know. Suddenly, I find people who genuinely want to help me get smarter. This is the opposite of what my ego would like to do—to pretend I'm an expert and look down on others.

That doesn't mean I should ignore my instincts of "I could do this better," or perhaps more accurately, "I would do that differently." Just because I can see a better way of doing something doesn't mean everyone else wants to do it my way. Not everyone thinks like me, and that's a good thing. Still, I see simple ideas daily and try them out, like developing a way to keep paper towels in our adventure van from unraveling on bumpy dirt roads. Or with Gossamer Gear, creating backpacks and tents, or running my own engineering company.

Often, I just make things for myself. Like in my job as a dishwasher at Sparrow, it was hard to wash the pastry bags. They flopped around in the machine and didn't really get clean. So I designed a wire frame that fit inside the bag and clicked into the dishwasher tray. *Voilà*, now both the insides and outsides of the bags get cleaned! I made a couple of these frames for my own use, but then a staff member from another location saw them and he wanted a couple for his use. That's how this entrepreneurial thing gets going.

Some entrepreneurs have a hard time working for other people, probably because they think they can do everything better. I've never had a problem working for others and have been a good employee many times in my life. Realistically, you're always working for someone else. If you own the company, you're working for your clients, your employees, and sometimes the bank and/or investors too. When you work for someone else, your main job is to make them look good, although usually that means you're doing a good job of serving others inside and outside the organization as well. Whenever I am working, in my mind, I'm working for myself. I'm always an employee of Glen Van Peski Inc. Most of the time, I have higher standards than the person signing my paycheck, and that has worked in my favor. As the majority shareholder of Glen Van Peski Inc., I take responsibility for my own training and development and for adding value to the organization.

Now that I've retired from a full-time career, I still find ways to challenge and occupy myself, like learning foreign languages. I've always loved languages (though I claim no special affinity) and so I've been keeping busy studying French, Italian, German, and Japanese. Over time, though, I came to see that Japanese is pretty difficult. I decided to focus my energies, then, on the other languages and watched as the dream of being even somewhat conversant in Japanese faded into the background. It would have been nice had I been able to master it, but my time would be better spent on other activities. Did I fail at learning Japanese? Not completely, because I know some phrases and understand more about the culture and language—little things I can use to build community the next time I'm in Japan. But I did not achieve what I set out to, so in that sense, I failed.

I love the scene in *Calvin and Hobbes* when Calvin sees a weight limit sign for a bridge their family car is about to cross and asks his father, "How do they know the load limit on bridges, Dad?"

His father replies, "They drive bigger and bigger trucks over the bridge until it breaks. Then they weigh the last truck and rebuild the bridge." Meanwhile, his mother quietly counsels the father. "Dear, if you don't know the answer, just tell him!"

More to the point, though, is this quote from Thomas Edison: "I have not failed. I just found 10,000 ways that won't work."[8]

This idea has always resonated with me, and I can see the hallmarks of its influence as I look back over my life and career choices as well as at my efforts at going ultralight when in the backcountry. If we're not constantly pushing the boundaries of what we know and how we're interacting with the world around us, then life becomes repetitive and tedious. There's so much more to see and understand, whether it's in how we pack our backpack, or how we learn to show our spouse how much they mean to us, or how we get up and brush ourselves off after we fall.

Many of us, though, avoid trying new things because we're afraid of failing. It may have been drilled into us somewhere in our past that failure is disgraceful and to be avoided at all costs.

The Stanford psychologist Carol Dweck coined the term *fixed mindset* to describe this way of seeing the world. A fixed mindset is the belief that our skills and abilities were set at birth and are unchangeable. We're stuck with what we got. We are who we are, and we'd best play up our strengths and stay away from our weaknesses unless we want to make fools of ourselves. People with fixed mindsets tend to avoid challenges and are terrified of failure. Failure, to them, is not an opportunity for growth but a reflection on their inherent abilities (or inabilities)—facts they'd rather the larger world not see. So they stick to the tried and true, what they know how to do and can do well, certain that to stray from what's safe is to invite shame.

I'd argue alongside Carol Dweck for the opposite, which she describes as having a *growth mindset*. This centers on a belief that abilities and traits can be developed through effort and learning. People with a growth mindset embrace challenges and see failure as only a temporary setback on the path to success. Because, after all, failure is where we learn so much—who we are as humans, our limits, and what matters to us. A growth mindset assumes we all have the ability to grow and master new tasks and abilities. Shying away from failure robs us of opportunities to grow and prevents us from knowing more about who we are and what we can do.

PEOPLE WITH FIXED MINDSETS TEND TO AVOID CHALLENGES AND ARE TERRIFIED OF FAILURE.

But don't worry if you believe you have a fixed mindset. Even that can change if you open yourself to the possibility of a growth mindset! In her important work *Mindset: The New Psychology of Success,*[9] Dweck not only explored the impact these two ways of thinking have on personal and academic achievement but also developed a way of fostering a growth mindset that can lead to success and fulfillment. Fixed mindsets need not stay fixed, she found, but to get over that fear of failure, we have to make peace with it and what it means.

For me, before I can embrace an activity that may lead to failure—designing a new piece of equipment, say, or starting my own company, learning a new language, or taking up an unfamiliar hobby, even starting to wash dishes at Sparrow Bakery—I have to remind myself of the upsides that come with failure. That way, if my plan ends up heading in that direction, I won't be too discouraged. This immediate failure is just a stepping stone along my path to an even bigger success.

These are the facts I remind myself of when I start getting weak-kneed at the idea of failing:

- When I fail, I develop increased resilience. If I understand that failure is a normal part of growth and development, then my ability to bounce back from setbacks increases and my capacity to succeed is enlarged.
- I also hone my problem-solving skills because failure provides me with opportunities to identify and analyze the root problems I'm facing. By getting good at this analysis, I'm better able to avoid failures in the future since my ability to assess the problems I face has become sharper.
- My creativity is also enhanced since every single act of failure can, if I allow it, lead to new and resourceful solutions to the problems I face.
- I gain when I fail because I come to understand better my own strengths and weaknesses. People who don't shy away from the failures but use them to better understand their strengths and weaknesses experience increased self-awareness and personal growth.
- Even when I fail, I meet people and make connections that may help me, or them, in the future. And how I conduct myself adds to my reputation, which can also be useful in future endeavors.

- And finally, facing failure and learning to overcome it can be a powerful motivator, giving us a boost that transcends the problem currently facing us. When we look back on all we've overcome, we remember that we have the intelligence and skill set to triumph over whatever perplexes us at the moment.

I recently read in the *Wall Street Journal* an article about the CEO of Overstock.com who set aside a day each week so that employees could eat lunch with him and ask him whatever they liked, a way of giving back to the community. I had done something similar back when I was community development director at the city of Carlsbad, offering to pay for lunch for anyone who wanted to spend that time with me, talking about whatever they wanted, and even allowing the question-asker to take my fun little Mini Cooper for a spin if they felt like it. But like the CEO of Overstock, I found myself mostly eating alone. Very few took me up on the offer, an opening that I would have grabbed earlier in my own career. I am not sure why more people do not take advantage of such opportunities. Is it a fear of failure or a fear of being exposed as not having all the answers? What I do know is that I had some great conversations with the people who did take me up on the offer and I'm still in touch with some of them today.

Just this morning, I ran into a woman I used to work with at Sparrow. A year or so ago, she'd asked to meet with me. She wanted to start her own business, and someone knew the old guy washing dishes had been pretty successful and had started a few businesses of his own. We went through the ins and outs of what it would take for her to launch her own bakery. She's now following through on her dream and is thriving.

When I ran into her this morning, I told her the Overstock story, and she, too, shook her head. She didn't understand it. "A bunch of the staff at Sparrow all had ideas for products they'd like to make or businesses they'd like to start, but none, besides me, wanted to sit down with you and ask about how to do it," she said.

Not that I have all the answers, but I've come to accept the fact that embracing what we don't know is often the first step toward success. Anyone you talk to can be helpful. If they don't have any knowledge that helps on your quest, they might know someone who does. And my experience is that generally, people like to help!

Remain Open

WHEN I RETIRED FROM MY CIVIL ENGINEERING JOB A FEW YEARS ago, so many people who knew me worried I'd be bored out of my skull without my regular routine. I've always been way too tied into the idea of being productive and getting stuff done. How was that going to work if I was retired?

I would say that so far it's working out pretty well. And I think maybe I've cracked the code, at least for me, not only for orchestrating a fulfilling retirement but for crafting an enriching life, whether I'm working or not.

I've found that when people think about retirement, they often focus on the things they don't like about work and that they'll finally be able to escape those things. I always advise people to spend some time thinking about the *good* things about work that they won't have anymore in retirement. For me, the aspects of work I enjoyed the most were how the work schedule provided a structure to hang tasks on and be productive, how work provided a place where I interacted with some people for ten to twenty years and built relationships, and how it gave me a chance to be part of a team, working together toward defined objectives.

I got some great advice before retiring, which was to not commit to anything for the first year. But gradually, I found a way to adapt to retirement life by capturing those elements of work that I enjoyed. For instance, when I first retired, I needed to figure out ways to create enough structure in my daily life to give me that satisfaction of accomplishment. Preparing and training for outdoor adventures took up some of that slack. And along the way, I learned to remain open to possibilities that showed up despite my best planning.

If I were still working full time today, I think the attitude of staying available to those elements that were not in the plan would have served me well.

Much of this lesson came home to me after one particular adventure.

It all started when I was talking with my neighbor Mike in the alley one day. Most of the houses here in the Northwest Crossing neighborhood of Bend have alleyways to allow folks to access their behind-the-house garages without making the street look like a row of garages. So many subdivisions are created with garages all facing the street because it's an efficient way for a builder to maximize density. But it tends to be ugly, and you end up with a streetscape that's just a ton of concrete driveways and garage doors. Plus, you never see your neighbors because they drive into their homes and are hidden from sight. I heard someone say the other day that they thought the automatic garage door opener was single-handedly responsible for the breakdown of community in America. I'm not sure that person was wrong.

Where we live now, we have alleys, and they give us twice as many opportunities to meet our fabulous neighbors. Not only do we discover wonderful friends who share the street-side of our home, both beside our place and across the street, but we also develop alley-way neighbors, those across the way in the back. Because there is limited traffic in the alleys, people wander up and down with their dogs, and kids play in the alleys instead of the streets. It is a great way to get to know folks. Mike Travis, who was about my age and recently retired, was one of my favorite "alley cats."

We were chatting one evening, late in the fall, about a possible mountain lion sighting in the area. Mike's a big skier and cyclist, and I don't remember how we got on the subject, but he let me know he had a hankering.

"I don't know, Glen. I'm a little bored. I'm itching, you know. I need a big adventure, maybe one on my bike." His voice was wistful.

"I told you about when I crossed the country on my bike when I was eighteen?"

"You did, and it's got me yearning in a bad way. But I'm not eighteen anymore. How many adventures can I possibly have left? I want to do something big, but I don't know exactly what. Or how."

"You're talking to the wrong person if you think I'm going to do anything besides urge you to follow through. Anything in particular you have in mind?"

"Well…" He seemed hesitant to tell me what he'd been thinking. "I've been reading about the Great Divide Mountain Bike Route for years. But, to be honest, it's a bit daunting, especially for someone my age. I wouldn't even know where to start."

At the time, I had never heard of that route, but he piqued my curiosity.

Established in 1997 by Adventure Cycling Association, the Great Divide Mountain Bike Route (GDMBR) is not marked by signs on the ground but by GPS coordinates that follow the general path of the Continental Divide of the Americas all the way from Banff, Canada, to New Mexico, traversing through Montana, Idaho, Wyoming, and Colorado along the way, covering more than twenty-seven hundred miles. Primarily on dirt and gravel roads and mountain trails, the route passes through a number of remote areas with limited services. It's considered one of the most challenging off-road cycling routes in the world. And that was the very reason Mike was tentative about taking on the challenge. I could understand his hesitancy but could also picture a way around it. A few days later, I saw him again in the alley.

"I looked it up, Mike. I don't really have specific knowledge of the GDMBR, but I've done a bunch of big trips. I probably don't know any more than you do, but I do know we're smart and we can figure it out together. Besides, one big trip is much like any other; we'll just adjust what I've done for previous trips and stay flexible. What do you say?"

"Really? Wow. Okay." There was a new glint in his eye. "Let's get this show on the road!"

It was coming into the dead of winter in Bend, and that gave us time to prepare. Soon, Mike created an amazing spreadsheet, based on the guidebook, and researched start dates. He thought a daily average of thirty to fifty miles, using the stages from the guidebook, seemed about right for old guys like us. We also had to time our departure just right so there wouldn't be too much snow on the passes.

We approached the trip as a thru-hiker would approach, say, the Pacific Crest Trail, with plans to mail ourselves resupply boxes of food along the way, generally carrying only four or five days of food on our bikes, along with tents and sleeping bags, and filtering water from streams along the way.

Our planning, though, was complicated due to COVID. This was early 2020, and we soon learned that many of the post offices in the little towns along the way, where we'd planned to pick up our resupply boxes, now had limited operating hours. Our resupply boxes could be received in a town of, say, sixty people, so the post office there might be open from only about eleven to two each day. Many places where we had thought we would enjoy a restaurant meal had closed down completely or were open only a day or two a week. We'd have to get the timing just right. Planning ahead under these circumstances was tricky. Stay flexible, we reminded ourselves. That would be the secret.

We also realized we'd have to scale down the length of the trip, partly because Canada was still inaccessible due to COVID restrictions.

Finally, we settled on our plan. We'd drive to Jackson, Wyoming, and leave one car there. Then we would drive to Eureka, Montana, a tiny town near the Canadian border; leave the second car there; and bike down to Jackson, Wyoming, a trip of about nine hundred miles. That felt big enough to both of us to give us the satisfaction we were each craving.

As we compiled our spreadsheets and looked out the window at the drifts of snow piling up, we encouraged each other.

"Don't you worry, Glen. That snow's gonna melt eventually," Mike said, a new energy swelling with an adventure in the offing.

But this is the nature of planning. You do all you can to take the guesswork out, and you never know what's going to happen, if the plan will hold. The success of a trip should never be judged by how well you were able to hew to the blueprint but rather how flexible you were in finding solutions to the obstacles you faced. Can we remain calm and focused, still seeing all the beauty around us, when things don't go as planned?

As they say, "Man plans, and God laughs." Can we learn to laugh too?

Sure enough, the snow started to melt, and the roads became passable enough for me to get some training miles in on the bike. Frankly, I was a bit worried about the fact I wasn't in the greatest shape, and I knew I needed to log some serious mileage before our June departure date arrived or I'd be in a world of hurt. When I was eighteen, it had been no big deal to figure I'd get in shape along the way. Not so much when you're in your sixties.

We were only a few weeks away from the trip, the food not yet packed and mailed, but getting super close, when I went out to ride on my own, become reacquainted with the bike, get my butt used to being in the saddle without feeling too bruised, and refamiliarize myself with maneuvering a fully loaded bike.

I'd ridden about twenty-five miles in the Deschutes National Forest west of Bend and was coming down a sketchy, long-abandoned logging path, back to the road that would eventually take me home. The path had deep ruts on either side and was kind of high in the middle. The whole area was overgrown and a bunch of fist-size rocks were lodged in the two ruts, so I was trying to stay on the high part. That was hard because I had to balance and move with precision on a fully loaded bike. The incline was steep coming down, so I hit the brakes, trying not to skid until I could navigate to the bottom where everything leveled out and the current logging operation was located.

WHEN I WAS EIGHTEEN, IT HAD BEEN NO BIG DEAL TO FIGURE I'D GET IN SHAPE ALONG THE WAY. NOT SO MUCH WHEN YOU'RE IN YOUR SIXTIES.

I heaved a sigh of relief when I got to that place. That had been gnarly, but now I was almost home free. And so I relaxed.

Rule number one when doing this kind of thing? Never relax.

The path was more level now, and where the ruts had previously been filled with rocks, they now were clear, and I assumed they'd make for easy going. Wrong. The minute my front tire hit the right-side rut, I knew I was in trouble. What looked like soil was actually deep dust created by the actions of the heavy machinery used in logging, which gave absolutely no support or traction. My tire dropped in and stopped, and I went flying over the handlebars.

I was on the ground, surprised to find myself there. I had been fine just a minute ago. How had this happened? I tried to sit up and realized my left arm hurt badly. Moving gingerly to not aggravate the pain, I got up, dusted myself off, and picked up my bike to examine it. It was dirty, but I didn't see anything broken. That was good.

My arm hurt too much to try to ride, so I decided I'd have to walk it out. But first, I needed to gather myself. I walked, shakily, to the shade of a juniper and pulled out my cell phone to see if I had service. Throughout much of the ride, I knew I'd be in areas with no service, so I was relieved to see I had one bar. I pulled up a map that showed me all the Forest Service roads and tried to figure out if I could give Francie directions to find me. With limited service, I wasn't going to be able to talk with her as she made her way to me, so I needed to identify a place we could easily find each other. The map I was looking at, meanwhile, hadn't been updated in a few years and I didn't know the conditions of the road, if they were even passable in a standard car. There was really no choice. I'd have to ride my way down the three and a half miles to where the road intersected the path. Somehow.

"I fell and am hurt. I need you to come get me." I told her to drive to the bridge over Tumalo Creek at the end of Skyliners Road, then continue along the gravel Forest Service Road 4603 until she found me. "Take my car because you'll need the extra space for the bike."

Francie doesn't get thrown by things like injuries, thanks to her background as a nurse, so she stayed calm and cool.

I mounted my bike, keeping most of my weight on my right arm, but the gravel road was really hard and uneven, and I needed my left hand on the grip to help steer. I screamed in pain and swore more in those three and a half miles bouncing down that road than I probably had in my sixty years prior. It was brutal.

When I got to Road 4603, she wasn't there. Given how close it was to the house, she should have been there long ago. I hadn't realized that she'd first have to find my keys. I'd also forgotten that I'd put my non-snow tires in the back of my car to have them changed out. To have room for my bike, she'd also need to unload all that. But I tried to stay positive. Frankly, it was a miracle I'd reached her in the first place because, back then as now, her phone was usually turned off. The only thing I could do now was to head down Road 4603 toward the bridge, figuring I would eventually run into her.

When I skittered down the last hill to the bridge, Francie pulled up. I was just standing there, barely able to hold myself upright. Francie fussed around, trying to load my bike, and all I could think (but didn't say) was, *If you don't get this bike loaded and me in a seat in like thirty seconds, I'm gonna pass out.* The pain was getting worse, and I was starting to realize I was in trouble.

When we got home, Francie took off my shirt, and I wished I hadn't seen what I saw in the mirror, bones jutting out in directions they're not supposed to go. My shoulder was clearly not okay. I knew it hurt like hell, but I hadn't realized it was that bad. Later, Francie's friends asked her if she'd cut my shirt off.

"No," she replied. "I would never cut that off. It was one of his favorite ultra-marathon shirts."

I took a shower because I was filthy from being face-down in the dust, and Francie fed me lunch because I was starving, and then we went to the ER, but Francie couldn't come in with me because of COVID precautions.

"How'd this happen?" the intake ER nurse asked.

I explained I hadn't been doing anything heroic, just riding down a dirt road.

"Well, there's still time to make up a good story," she said.

They took X-rays and determined I had a distal break in my collarbone that would likely need surgery. After I was given a referral to an orthopedic surgeon, they said I could go.

"Did they give you anything for pain?" Francie asked when she picked me up.

"They offered, but I said 'nah.' It doesn't hurt that bad."

At work at the Sparrow Bakery

The famed 2019 trip through Buckskin Gulch, with Ali Selim, Dan Buettner, me, Edward Driscoll, Matthew McConaughey, Bill Weir, Ben Graves, David McLain (Photo: David McLain)

Rose wearing the jacket McConaughey used in Buckskin Gulch

My son Brian and me on a Boy Scouts trip in the
Sierra, c. 1996 (PHOTO: READ MILLER)

The G4 pack—the one
that started it all

My third pack, the G3, c. 1997

Cyclists touch New Castle
on cross-country journey

How far can four people go in six days? Four Massachusetts youths pedaled their knapsack-laden 10-speeds from Amherst, Mass., to New Castle in that time.

The boys, Mark Howards, Guy Holappa, Glenn Van Peski and Todd Sunderland, between age 16 and 19, are bound for San Francisco.

The four told Mr. and Mrs. John Hudson of 427 E. Leasure Ave. that they had plans of getting to San Francisco by Aug. 1.

According to Mrs. Hudson, who saw the boys on Friday afternoon at Burger Chef, the youths left their homes in Amherst, Mass., on June 12. They plan to cross the northern part of the

country, traveling through Wyoming and that area, then heading south toward San Francisco," she said. While traveling, the boys said they plan to stay with friends or to camp out.

After arriving in San Francisco, they will fly home to Amherst, having their bicycles shipped.

According to Mrs. Hudson, both she and her husband, an insurance man who happened to have a polaroid camera in his car at the time, are bicycle enthusiasts. However, she said, they have never planned a cross country trip.

"Maybe sometime," she said, "but Massachusetts to California is an awfully ambitious trip."

FOUR FOR THE ROAD — Four boys, from left, Mark Howards, Guy Holappa, Glenn Van Peski and Todd Sunderland, all from Amherst, Mass., passed through New Castle Friday on their way to San Francisco. The boys plan to reach their destination by Aug. 1. Their bikes, they have announced, will be shipped home.

Newspaper article from New Castle, PA,
detailing my 1976 bike trip across the US

Carrying both my and Francie's packs, Buckskin Gulch

Testing a water belt with a sub-3 lb. base weight on the PCT, 2006

Me on a trip in the Emigrant Wilderness, 2022 (PHOTO: DUNCAN CHEUNG)

Brain Trust Hike by early ultralight backpacking gear company founders in the Cascades, 2011: Henry Shires (Tarptent), Brian Frankle (ULA), Ron Moak (Six Moon Designs), me (Gossamer Gear)

The wreckage from the plane crash that I survived, 1987

The prank magazine cover featuring Francie's bathroom
decorating skills (PHOTO: BRIAN VAN PESKI)

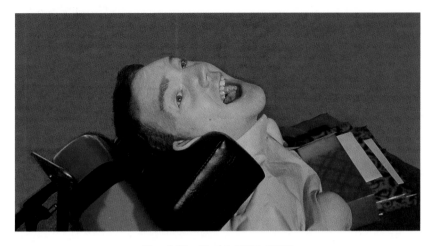

Derek Van Peski, 1987–2007

The yellow-lined pad recording the first orders of the fledgling GVP Gear

Mike Travis and me on our 2022 bikepacking trip
along the Great Divide Mountain Bike Route

Hiring notice similar to the one that started me
down the career path of dishwashing

Diane with Jenny and Francie, Buckskin Gulch, 2015

Francie and me at home in Bend, 2023

Just another day as a cowgirl for Amelia, Miss Montana (Runner Up), 2021

Grant Van Peski enjoying trail magic on the PCT, 2003

Boondocking in Wally, above Ely, Nevada

Backstage at the local news station in Bend. They're wearing my ties!

Francie and me on our wedding day, 1982

Speaking to 100+ people at the Adventure 16 store in San Diego, August 2002. The store had estimated 12 to 15 people would show up.

Me, Brian, Francie, and Grant, 2022

Gossamer Gear CEO Jonathan Schmid, president Grant Sible,
and me (founder) at Outdoor Retailer (PHOTO: CARLO NASISSE)

In Golden Trout Wilderness on a three-day trip with just a lumbar pack, 2015

Me showing early affinity for washing dishes. Here I am with
my mom, Claire, who probably had no idea her firstborn
son would end up washing dishes professionally.

The Gossamer Gear team in 2022 in front of the Congress Street offices: David, Rhett, Sarah, Gracie, me, Francie, and Jonathan. (Not pictured: Grant)

Stuck in quicksand, Buckskin Gulch (Photo: Diane Arnold)

With friends in Japan, preparing to backpack in Chichibu Wilderness, 2010

Reflection in the shadow of the Matterhorn,
Zermatt, Switzerland (Photo: Grant Sible)

"That's because you're in shock. When the shock wears off, you're going to be hurting something awful."

"Really?"

"Really. Rule number one: never refuse a script. You don't have to fill it, but you'll have it later if you need it."

With that, she called the ER back. "My husband wasn't thinking clearly. We'll take that prescription after all."

Later, I was glad she had. I had surgery five days later, and I told Mike we had to postpone our big trip until the following year, which was a hard blow to both of us.

But a year later, we finally got to do it. I think maybe we appreciated the trip even more because of all it had taken in time, planning, and delays to get there. It was hard. Anytime you're doing something like that day after day after day, it takes a toll on the body that you don't experience doing day rides. Plus, we were sleeping on the ground every night and never felt fully rested. That said, we had an experience on the trek that put our little aches and pains into perspective.

We'd pulled up to Holland Lake campground in the Flathead National Forest in Montana, and the host said there was only one site left, so we took it. We had leaned our bikes against our site's picnic table and were in the process of unpacking when a young man approached. "We're supporting this gal who's doing this trek on a handcycle," he explained. "The camp host says you two got the last campsite available. Would it be okay if we shared yours?" He sealed the deal with a couple of cold beers.

It turned out that he and his crew were the chase vehicle, food makers, and general auxiliary provision system for Quinn Brett, a young woman who'd been paralyzed three years earlier in a rock-climbing fall on El Capitan in Yosemite. She was now doing the route we were, but the whole enchilada—twenty-seven hundred miles versus our nine hundred—on an e-assisted hand cycle. Compared to what she was going through and the struggles and obstacles she faced, our little aches and pains seemed minor.[10]

I'm not a fan of using someone else's disability as a form of inspiration. While highlighting the achievements of someone who's disabled can be empowering, it can also turn people from actual humans into patronized and dehumanized objects. Doing so often perpetuates the myth that a person with a disability needs to triumph over adversity to be a valued member of society. As the father of Derek, who'd been so profoundly disabled his entire life, it is important to me to recognize the inherent value and worth of all people, regardless of one's abilities or disabilities.

I FELT A WHOLE NEW LEVEL OF RESPECT FOR WHAT DETERMINATION CAN ACHIEVE AND REALIZED HOW PIDDLING MY OWN CHALLENGES ON THIS TRIP HAD BEEN.

But wow. Seeing what Quinn was doing, I felt a whole new level of respect for what determination can achieve and realized how piddling my own challenges on this trip had been. While I think of myself as someone who's naturally kind of stoic, just putting one foot in front of the other, Mike had long described himself as a whiner, confessing that "This is hard" was his favorite retort.

But I think he didn't want to come off as complaining during this trip, so while he may have been thinking *This is hard* inside himself most of the way, he pulled up all his courage and just kept going. We both did. But seeing what Quinn was experiencing made me realize that even my stoic stance held nothing to her heart and grit.

When all was said and done, we made it back home safely and had lots of stories to tell. Sitting around after, having a beer, I asked Mike where this adventure fit for him on the Fun Scale. Had he seen the trip as Type I Fun, defined as enjoyable as it's happening? A great meal at a restaurant, a lovely hike—it's what we imagine when we plan such trips. Or maybe for him it was Type II Fun, which may not be enjoyable as it's happening but you feel great about it after the fact, like doing an ultramarathon or parenting teenagers. Type III Fun is a total misnomer because it's not fun at all, even in retrospect. More like, "What the hell were we thinking?" This type of fun provides zero enjoyment but a bunch of crazy stories, though they're usually of the "cautionary tale—don't try this at home" variety.

The thing about the Fun Scale is that experiences are subjective and often change over time. When we were out there on a rainy, muddy day and had run low on food and nothing was going as planned, he might have called it Type III. But now at home, having slept in a comfy bed for a number of nights and having had some good meals and hot showers, the perspective changed. As our memories of suffering faded, what might have been Type III morphed into Type II. "It wasn't all that bad," he said. "What'll we plan next?"

None of which would have happened if both Mike and I hadn't stayed open to the idea of having an experience in the first place. We tried not to prejudge what we were doing, to make it into something it wasn't. Good, bad, or indifferent, we were open to what was in store for us, and that, I think, is a great lesson I can apply to all parts of my life.

Besides being open to grand adventures in the wilderness far from home, it pays to be alert and open in daily life as well. When we first moved to Bend, I celebrated my retirement by walking to nearby Sparrow Bakery every Monday morning with my *Wall Street Journal* and my Ember mug. I would happily spend an hour or two sipping coffee, savoring a decadent Ocean Roll, reading the paper, and rejoicing that I wasn't at my desk at the office at 5:00 a.m. Being at Sparrow on a regular basis gave me an opportunity to watch the staff in action and get to know a few of them by name. I was impressed at how they all seemed to be having a good time, backing each other up, working as a team. And from snippets of overhead conversations, I could tell that, in many cases, the relationships extended to outside of work hours.

One morning as I was leaving, I noticed a sign on the exit door: "Attention High Schoolers, we're looking for a part-time dishwasher." I didn't pay much attention, because high school was a *long* way in my rearview mirror, and I wasn't looking for a job since I had just retired from one.

After weeks of seeing that sign, I asked at the counter, "Hey, don't you guys need to take that sign down?" I figured it couldn't be *that* hard to hire a part-time dishwasher. They explained that they wanted to find the right person, and they weren't in a rush. It turns out that Rainger, an outdoor enthusiast who played in a local band and had taken over dishwashing on Mondays to give a day off to Maria, the diminutive powerhouse who was the main dishwasher the rest of the week, was headed to Belize for an extended vacation, and someone was needed to cover his Mondays while he was gone.

The more I thought about that sign, the more I thought that maybe God had my name on it. I liked having a regular work schedule since it oriented the rest of my weeks as well. I also enjoyed being part of a functioning team. Plus I was new to Bend, so I figured working at one of the neighborhood's most popular hangouts would be a great way to get to know the area, especially people I might not have a chance to meet otherwise.

So the next Monday, I asked for an application. Rainger asked, "For who?" assuming I had a grandson or nephew in mind.

"For me," I said.

He shrugged and said to submit the completed application with a copy of my résumé. I thought about my résumé: summa cum laude degree in engineering, master's in business, started multiple companies, was a professional registered engineer in three Western states as well as a licensed land surveyor. "You know, I have to admit that my résumé is a little light on the professional dishwashing experience," I conceded.

Rainger patted my shoulder. "I wouldn't worry about it. I've noticed we like to teach people *our* way to do things."

The day of the interview arrived. It was snowy by this time of year. As I said, though I hadn't been interviewed much, I knew you dressed up for the occasion. Thankfully, I hadn't ditched all my business clothes when I retired, and I was ready to do what one should always do for an interview: go all in! So I donned my French cuffs with gold cuff links, custom wool suit, tie, and neatly-folded pocket square. I laced my wingtips and headed over through the snow. When I arrived, one of the Sparrow employees recognized me. "Glen, you're looking a little different today than usual!"

"I'm here for my interview," I beamed.

He laughed. "Take a seat. Whitney will come out when she has a chance."

When Whitney and I sat down, I explained that I understood I would not be washing dishes dressed in a suit. But when I found out I would be interviewing with an owner instead of the site manager, I wanted to show proper respect for what she and Jess had created. Establishing good morale and a smooth-running machine usually starts at the top, I noted. We chatted about the position, and I ended up getting hired. As it turned out, I got to work even before Rainger left for Belize when the kid who washed dishes Sunday morning broke his wrist snowboarding (an occupational hazard in an outdoor-oriented place like Bend).

It was great being part of a team. And it was great bringing home bags of leftover pastries at the end of my shifts, which I distributed on my way home. I would walk back to our house, texting neighbors. They figured out quickly to have their cell phones turned on and near them on Monday afternoons so I didn't pass them over for the next neighbor on the list. These days I just work a shift here and there to cover if someone gets sick or is on vacation. I have plenty of other projects, and we travel a lot, so it works out. And the neighbors have probably lost a pound or two since I stopped working quite as regularly. But I stop to think: if I hadn't noticed that sign and been curious about it, I might have missed out on all the richness in my life that has flowed from washing dishes at The Sparrow Bakery. Remaining aware of what's around you, and open to what it might mean in your life, can lead to some very rewarding experiences.

LESSON 13

Keep Making Friends

SIX DEGREES OF KEVIN BACON, ALSO KNOWN AS BACON'S LAW, IS a parlor game that became popular in the 1990s when, in an interview with a magazine, then-prolific actor Kevin Bacon mentioned that he had worked with everybody in Hollywood or someone who's worked with them. Upon reading that comment, fans posited that Kevin Bacon was actually "The Center of the Hollywood Universe," because everyone seemed to be connected to him.

The way to play the game is to arbitrarily choose an actor and then connect them to another actor via a film that both actors appeared in together, repeating this process to discover the shortest path that ultimately leads back to Kevin Bacon. Indeed, following the rules of this game, we can see how it works with actor Matthew McConaughey. McConaughey was featured in the film *Interstellar* with William Devane, who was in the film *Hollow Man* with Kevin Bacon. Thus, McConaughey is separated from Kevin Bacon by only two links.

The truth is, we're all connected to each other by far fewer steps than we realize, a theory known as six degrees of separation and also known as the "small world" phenomenon. This theory holds that any two people on this planet are six or fewer social connections away from each other. And while some people joke in the backcountry hiking world you could play Six Degrees of Glen Van Peski, it's really not so odd to find out we're often only an introduction or two away from knowing some of the world's most amazing, interesting people.

I had long known this but became even more fully inspired by the intriguing people I met on hikes organized by John Mackey, the Whole Foods guy. He always pulled together a diverse and delightfully odd group, with folks from different ages, genders, races, and socioeconomic statuses, representing the arts, commerce, government, you name it. Some were multi-millionaires, a few were PhD geniuses; in the mix was also an itinerant cowboy who was the first in his family to graduate high school. This blending together of people outside of those I might meet on a regular basis, I found, was an enriching experience and showed me how much there was to gain from knowing people from other spheres.

But I knew this kind of comingling would take active work. Left to my own devices, I'd end up with the same or similar group of people as I always had, and yet there was so much more for me to learn in meeting those from outside my limited social circle.

So ten years ago, I decided to put in the time and effort to explore this idea, and I called the project "The List." This would be a compendium of strangers I had met throughout the year who I would then invite on a trip—like the one I described in Lesson 1— so we could all make connections with one another. The aim was to connect with as many different people as possible to ensure I was in the swim of life and not hiding out in the protected shallows where everyone looked like me and thought like me; to force me to be open to new connections, new ways of seeing the world, and to make myself fully available to as many opportunities in this lifetime as I might have.

Throughout the year, I noted down the names of people whose paths I had crossed only tangentially but whom I might want to get to know better. Or, just as importantly, those who might benefit from knowing someone else I knew.

I would ask those named on this initial version of The List to come on an arduous trip with me and five or six others—to Buckskin/ Paria or on a similar adventure. To do so, I needed to identify the criteria for who should be on The List.

The first criteria, which was the most important and absolutely nonnegotiable, was that the person should be good company on the trail. I captured this quality via this shorthand expression: "People who have something to say but nothing to prove."

This first criteria had several facets. I was looking for people who had led interesting lives, which I quickly found, if I was paying attention, was pretty much everyone. I was hoping to identify people who were willing both to share their experiences with each other and to help shoulder the burden of what's required for such an outing.

The people I chose were also interested in listening to others tell their own stories. I found it enriching to talk with these people, not just about what they'd experienced in life but also about their hobbies, how they thought about things, current issues. I wanted to see the world from as many different perspectives as possible.

Since I was hoping to build groups that worked well with each other, I also wanted to find people who didn't need to be the center of attention all the time and might suck up all the oxygen. Even with a famous actor like Matthew McConaughey, who's a consummate storyteller, I found that despite telling great stories himself, he was also interested in hearing from the other group participants. That was the dynamic I was after.

The second qualification was that the person should be reasonably fit and a strong hiker. While I can often vary the trips somewhat based on the final makeup of the participants, I tended to approach these trips from a thru-hiker mentality. Francie knows well my exhortation of "We're burnin' daylight," which loosely translates into "Pack up and let's get walking." This is because, while I'm retired, many people on The List are still working full time and have limited spaces on their calendar for outdoor adventure. To show them some of my favorite remote backcountry places, we'd need to get some steady miles in.

For many of the trips, the miles were dictated by the circumstances of the route. For example, on my annual Buckskin-Paria trip, once we leave the trailhead at Wire Pass, we have to slog sixteen-plus miles through Buckskin Gulch and down the Paria River to get to Big Spring, usually the first reliable water source. My companions and I all needed to be able to hike that distance in just one day or we'd potentially run out of water.

The final qualification was that they have their gear kit down pat. What they carry should be reasonably light if they're going to do the miles I set out, and they should know how to use it. They don't need to be expert backpackers, but my trips aren't designed for people who are new to the sport. While I'm happy to share a tip here and there on how to be a better backpacker, to be honest, I simply don't have the patience or expertise to do a systematic, organized, educational effort on backpacking. More recently, I have teamed with my friend Duncan Cheung, who runs Off Trail On Track, to do some trips for people who don't yet have the experience to make it onto The List. Duncan is a superb outdoorsman and a talented and patient educator, so he provides essentially a full course on backpacking.

These trips are regular occurrences, things I put on my calendar in advance. And I strive to always be inclined to near-strangers I might like to get to know better, those I pass on an average day whose life might enrich my own or who might be enriched themselves by this experience.

Often I meet people at speaking events who come up afterward to chat. From our brief conversation, I get a good feel for the person and sense they'd meet the criteria for The List. Sometimes I "meet" people who seem like good candidates for The List through an email exchange. For instance, Jeremy McAllister, a pastor in San Bernardino, started by emailing me with questions on ultralight backpacking. It was obvious he had given some thought to lightening his load and had a light kit already. We ended up doing a hike on a section of the Pacific Crest Trail together.

Later Jeremy laughed at how, four or five emails into our exchange, he realized I was "interviewing" him in a subtle way. I was trying to see if he'd be a good candidate for The List. Later, I invited Jeremy on the next Buckskin Gulch trip, and he was a joy, so enthusiastic. He kept exclaiming how many "firsts" the trip provided him: first time in a slot canyon, first time wading through freezing puddles, first time drinking water untreated directly from a spring, first time "cowboy camping" in the sand without a tent, first time encountering quicksand and its dangers.

I STRIVE TO ALWAYS BE INCLINED TO NEAR-STRANGERS I MIGHT LIKE TO GET TO KNOW BETTER, THOSE I PASS ON AN AVERAGE DAY WHOSE LIFE MIGHT ENRICH MY OWN OR WHO MIGHT BE ENRICHED THEMSELVES BY THIS EXPERIENCE.

It was also possible, I came to see after working this idea for some time, for a person to earn his or her way *off* The List. I usually have a pretty good feel for people, but I am sometimes wrong. One year on a trip, a young man turned out to be a parkour aficionado. On our hike, he was bouncing around the canyon walls, trying to avoid getting his feet wet, clambering up rock falls. In doing so, he focused solely on himself and put the group at risk. If he fell and got injured, he'd have to be evacuated and our whole outing would be ruined. He also could have knocked rocks down and injured one of our fellow travelers. Being so absorbed with his own desires, he was unable to see where and how he was posing harm to those around him. I crossed him off The List after that.

I also learned it was possible to earn your way off The List without ever actually going on a trip. One year, I met a man and his wife at a talk I gave for the Wilderness Basics Course in San Diego. They seemed nice, fit, and organized. I put them on The List and included them on that year's Buckskin Gulch invitation. The man was in a related leadership field, so we met for lunch one day. Over our meal, he revealed that he might not be able to make the trip because he had a doctor's appointment scheduled during that time frame. I didn't want to pry but wondered if it was a medical condition to be concerned with.

"Oh, heavens no!" He waved away my worry. "I just like to get an annual physical to keep on top of my health, and it's hard to get an appointment. If I cancel, I'll have to call every day to see if I could get another spot."

Right then, I decided that prioritizing an annual physical over a once-in-a-lifetime trip down a slot canyon to see never-before-witnessed vistas exhibited poor judgment—both on his part and on mine for including him on The List.

This is how I use The List. A couple of times a year, I obtain six to eight permits for a favorite hike. Utah's Buckskin Gulch is a perennial choice, as is the Sierra High Country. Once I get those permits, I send out the dates to everyone on The List, currently about sixty people, to see who can make it. After that, it's first come, first served until all the permits are spoken for. Some folks on The List have been on multiple trips with me, though I typically give preference to first-timers for a particular location, while others have been on The List for years and we've never been able to make it work.

By using this technique, not only do I have a great trip and make new friends but those who go on these trips often bond with each other and then start doing trips of their own together. Others from The List now have their own lists, and the goodness keeps multiplying.

It makes sense. When organizers choose a location they're familiar with, they take a lot of the stress out of the planning for those who might like to go but would never do so on their own or without help. That organizer makes it easier for others to say yes to the invite. As a result, concentric circles of connection continue to be made.

I've been thinking for some time that I may need to create sub-lists for outings other than backpacking trips. A cruise could be one example where a few couples could have a good time and make new connections (in fact, we've been the recipient of a couple of just such invitations). We've also toyed with the idea of renting an eight-bedroom villa in Tuscany for a month and then sending out invites to a variant of The List for people to come spend a week.

I have also been the beneficiary of other people's planning, and I love that. Francie and I have taken several trips to Europe, each time with friends. When someone else does the heavy lifting in terms of setting the dates and getting accommodations—or at least for the common portions of the trips—then it makes it easy for us to participate. Not only that, but we develop great friendships and share those experiences with others.

And I've been amazed over and over again to see this "small world" phenomenon at work. Because of The List and other methods of connection, I often find myself surrounded by, or becoming connected to, amazing people.

For instance, Francie and I have a dear friend of thirty years, Diane. Six months after Francie gave birth to Derek and we were dealing with his health issues, Diane gave birth to her son Kevin, who had similar challenges but for different reasons. For months after Kevin was born, she kept running into people who told her she needed to meet Francie and me. It started to get ridiculous, the number of people who recommended she get in touch. Eventually we did connect and quickly became steadfast friends, nursing our disabled sons through the early days at home and then when they each went into outside care. Their journeys paralleled each other over and over again: Derek and Kevin were born six months apart, they entered formal care within six months of each other, and later, one died within six months of the other. And along the way, Francie and Diane supported each other every step.

Though Diane ran ultramarathons for years, it was somewhat later in life that she decided to give backpacking a try. I took her on a trip of The List to Buckskin Gulch, and she was hooked. She started planning her own trips, hauling her girlfriends on many adventures. She became a huge cheerleader for Gossamer Gear.

This one time, Diane was backpacking in the Sierra with a mutual friend. She was setting up her tent near a remote lake, high above a mountain pass, when she watched a young family—mother, father, and two children—clamber off the trail and proceed to set up their own equipment. Diane, who'd become quite a gearhead by this point, went over to ask about the gear they were carrying. It didn't look like others she had seen.

"That's a very different backpack," she observed. "And I haven't seen a tent like that before."

"I made them myself," the father proudly told her. "I became fascinated by the designs of this guy, Glen Van Peski. He started a company. Maybe you've heard of it, Gossamer Gear?"

Diane started laughing. "Oh my goodness! You have no idea. Glen is a dear friend."

"You *know* Glen Van Peski?"

"I more than know him. He and his wife, Francie, have been close to me and my family for thirty years."

The man couldn't get over his good luck. "Do you think you could make an introduction? I'd love to meet him."

"I would be honored to, but right now, Glen and Francie are not at home. I live in the San Diego area and they're not far from me. But they've decided to move and are out of state right now, building their new house."

"Oh." The man seemed crushed. "But there's no rush. I can wait. I'd really like to meet him. Where are they moving to?"

"Bend, Oregon," Diane told him.

"You must be kidding! We live in Bend!" he laughed.

It was an amazing coincidence—or was it? That very weekend, in fact, Francie and I were actually in Portland visiting Brian, and within a forty-eight-hour window, we had four or five wild "small world" experiences of our own. Maybe connections like this are all around us just waiting for us to see them. Later, that man and his family got to know us in Bend, and we have been enriched by their lives. Just as Diane's life, Kevin's and Derek's lives, and the lives of all who have touched ours have deepened our own lives.

We have so many "small world" experiences that I have to conclude that I walk by many people every day who I have some connection to, if I only take the time to explore it.

Are there people you'd like to invite to do something fun with you? It doesn't need to be a backpacking trek. Maybe you'd like to plan a game night at the local community center? A walking club? Perhaps run a community garden? Who would you put on your own list? What amazing links might just be waiting for you to take this step?

LESSON 14

Cultivate a Heart of Gratitude

Julie Andrews said the immortal words "enough is as good as a feast" to the children in her charge, Jane and Michael Banks, in the 1964 Disney movie *Mary Poppins*. That phrase has always struck me as deeply wise and insightful. Though the children in that movie had worries and aches of their own—not getting the attention they craved from their distracted parents, primarily—their lives were blessed in many ways. Mary Poppins was right: to have enough, and to *know* we have enough, is to be blessed many times over.

Like the children in that film, we must learn to consciously remind ourselves of our copious blessings even when the rest of our life doesn't measure up in the way we want. There will always be aches and wishes beyond our reach, and yet we can still appreciate what we have and share our plenty.

When I have approached life from this perspective of abundance, it has always been easier to see the goodness in the people I meet and to not feel the need to one-up them or assert myself in any way. When I see intrinsic value in others, first as a unique creation loved by God, then I can more easily pay attention to what that person brings to the table. Granted, with some folks, I have to work harder to see it than with others, but anytime I look hard enough, I can always find it.

Still, I'm abashed to realize that my achievements in life, such as they are, resulted in part from how advantaged I was from the get-go. I was born a straight, white male in the richest country in the world, with no major physical or emotional disabilities, and raised by loving, educated middle-class parents. When I think of it that way, I have to wonder why I haven't achieved more.

Many others have not had the advantages I have. A homeless man living in his car may have conquered far more hardship than I can even imagine, experiences I may not have been strong enough to survive. I need to keep that in mind regularly lest I start to become proud of what I've accomplished.

And while I have been blessed more than some others, I believe the purpose of those blessings is so I may bless others. I try to keep my eyes open for those opportunities.

The Ontiveros family comes to mind.

I don't remember where we first saw the information. Francie and I had just moved to Vista, California, and maybe it was on a billboard or in the newspaper, but the headline stuck in my brain: "Vista Caring and Sharing Program."

You've probably seen something similar in your neighborhood where an organization will pair you with a family in need for Thanksgiving or Christmas. You take them some foodstuffs and maybe some gifts for the children, just to help out on a personal level. Often, you're given a list of children, including their genders and ages, and pick out things for them that will be delivered by the organization. We signed up.

But instead of everything being done anonymously, as is common with many such organizations, in this setup we got to actually meet the family. And what a blessing that has been in our lives!

The Ontiveros parents were originally from Mexico and lived in a trailer park. They had two girls and a boy, who was the youngest. They worked hard to provide their kids opportunities they hadn't had. The dad did handyman and concrete work and had basically built the place they lived in, a plywood structure tacked onto the side of a travel trailer. The mom, Esperanza, had super bad arthritis, and her hands were pretty gnarled, which she never complained about. This wasn't a family living high on the hog, that's for sure, but the kids never went hungry, and they knew they were loved.

We signed up initially for Thanksgiving and got to know the family. It turns out the only reason they were in the Caring and Sharing program was that a neighbor had signed them up. The Ontiveros parents were proud of being able to support their own family and didn't want to accept charity from others. Soon, we became invested in their lives, and our interactions with each other went well beyond the objectives of the actual program.

We brought over gifts for Christmas and then the Ontiveros girls came to our home sometimes to babysit Brian and Grant so Francie and I could have a night out. The dad came over to install some tile in our bathroom. I guess what I'm trying to say is, we really got to know the family and became close to them. We learned about their circumstances and opened our hearts to them. The girls were both very, very bright, and we encouraged their education and stayed in touch as they grew up.

The middle child, Linda, eventually graduated high school. By that time I was a consultant working for the city of Carlsbad. Bob Wojcik, the deputy city engineer, was then trying to hire some office help to process the plans and permits and handle all the myriad paperwork. In order to hire someone, he needed to justify to senior management just how many man-hours were required, where the money would come from, and so on. I knew all this was happening in the background, but really, it wasn't my dilemma because I was a consultant, not an employee. I went about my work.

I came in one day, though, and he was clearly in a bad mood. "What's up?" I asked.

He gave me the lowdown, how he'd done all this work to justify a new position and yet his proposal had been rejected. "I really need the help and I don't know how to solve this issue."

I went home that night and thought about what he'd said. When I was in the office the next time, I made him a proposal.

"So Bob, you know my contract with the city is fairly general in its scope and it's well funded."

"Yup."

"And I know this outstanding young woman, Linda Ontiveros. She could do what you need and you'd be so lucky to have her. She's smart, hardworking, and—"

WHEN I'M NOT FOCUSED SOLELY ON MYSELF AND CAN ACTUALLY SEE THOSE AROUND ME AND WHERE THEY MIGHT BE IN NEED, IT'S LIKE SHARPENING THE FOCUS RING ON A PAIR OF BINOCULARS.

"I get it, Glen," he cut me off. "I'd love to hire someone like that. But the city's not going to budge. I can't pay her on good wishes alone."

"No, that's not what I'm suggesting. How's this: I'll hire her and then provide an extension of my staff to you?"

"I'm not sure I understand."

"Linda will become my employee, and I'll loan her services to you as needed. I'll pay her salary and you'll have the help you need."

"You'd do that?"

"Yup."

Here's the deal. When we help others in life, we add goodness all around. This move would allow me to help both Linda and Bob and cost me only a little financially—I billed the city for her time even though it took some funds from my contract. As I saw it, I was just trying to solve a problem for a client.

As a result, Linda came to work at the city as my employee for a year or two. She did such a fabulous job, and Bob was quite pleased. Armed with a work history with Linda, he was finally able to get her hired on the city's staff full time. It worked out well for everyone. Now Linda's got a good city job with full benefits, a real career, which is a blessing at the moment given the fact that her husband became unemployed, and he was able to stay home and do an amazing job raising their kids.

The reality is, I did almost nothing except connect people and try to see where I might be of service. Not a bad outcome over the course of nearly twenty years from seeing a call to participate in the Vista Caring and Sharing Program.

Where in your life might you add to the stream of life? Where do you have enough for a feast to which you might invite others?

I have to admit that learning to take time and mental energy away from our own pursuits to see where and how we might help others takes a little practice. But be assured: doing so pays off handsomely. When we step out of our little bubbles of self-absorption and see others where they are, listen to their woes, share their triumphs, and offer assistance where we can, we feel connected to others and recognize that our little efforts matter. And sometimes we're able to lighten someone else's load.

I think this is possible only when we fully realize just how blessed we are. Cultivating a heart of gratitude changes the entire world. When I'm not focused solely on myself and can actually see those around me and where they might be in need, it's like sharpening the focus ring on a pair of binoculars. I can see so much farther than with my unaided sight alone, and I come to recognize where I might add some goodness to this life.

Sometimes this lesson comes to me in small ways.

Like the time we were staying with Francie's dad's cousin Jim, who lives in Japan. He is married to Keiko, a Japanese woman he met while teaching English in Japan. We were there to visit him, yes, but also for me to give a talk on ultralight backpacking at a little coffee shop in Tokyo. Not only would my talk be translated but the organizers had also gone through my PowerPoint deck and changed my bullet points to Kanji.

Before Francie and I left for this speaking engagement, Jim pulled me aside.

"Glen, here's what's going to happen. After the talk, they're going to want to go out for drinks with you at an izakaya. But they're Japanese, so they're not going to say outright, 'Hey, you want to go for drinks?' That would be too forthright and bold in their culture. They will kind of walk around the idea for a while, hinting without asking for a long time. So I'm going to teach you the Japanese phrase *Hai! Nomitai desu*, which means, 'Yes! I want to go drinking.'"

I practiced the phrase with him a couple of times until I had it down, and then we took the train to the coffee shop. Posters and an item in the paper had been so successful in drawing participants that I had to give my talk twice to accommodate all who came to hear. When it was over and people were dispersing, one of the organizers, Terasawasan, who probably knew the most English of anyone there, came over to me.

"Great talks, Glen," he said. "We so appreciate that. And now, it's not too late tonight. Actually, it's still rather early. And we have a ride for you back home, so you don't need to worry about that, and there's this great little place, close to here, we could actually walk there, so we were wondering if maybe we could go there for a quick drink. What do you think?"

Thanks to Jim, I knew what he was hinting at. In my best Japanese accent (that was probably laughable to them all) I called out loudly, "*Hai! Nomitai desu!*"

Everyone laughed and clapped in joyful surprise, and Terasawasan gave me a big hug, which is not very Japanese. They were all so tickled.

And it was all thanks to the thoughtfulness of this cousin, who knew the awkwardness that might have come about and had the insight to prepare me. As it was, everyone was delighted by this tiny phrase I could utter, and it was fun to surprise them.

Which tells me that being kind and generous doesn't always have to cost us a lot. It's more a matter of attuning ourselves to those around us. But that takes practice, like everything else.

One Saturday in July, 2022, I was contacted by Henry at Food for the Sole, a mother-and-son operation in Bend that makes dehydrated, healthy vegan meals for backpackers.

"There's a woman here who's been doing the PCT as a thru-hike," Henry said. "She's hurt her foot and is taking a few days off to rest. She has some medical issues that have been complicated by the pack she's carrying. Any chance you could make her a custom one?"

"Not really, Henry," I said. "I just don't have the time. But maybe I could modify her existing pack."

"Great. I'll bring her over. Her name is Crystal Gail Welcome and she's attempting the Great Western Loop. She's a hiker of some renown and is carrying a Six Moon Designs pack."

After we hung up I went online to learn a little more. Turns out Crystal is a force of nature, working to help more Black, Indigenous, and People of Color (BIPOC) find a welcome in the outdoors, and encouraging others like herself to access all the bounty to be found in the backcountry. In a profile about her, she says, "Many people may recognize my name; I am a Black lesbian and thru-hiker with a neurological implant, and I am vocal about racial inequality in the outdoors."

It was interesting reading about her, and I was willing to see what I could do to help, but I wondered what she would be like in person. In my experience, sometimes people who are "activists" of some sort can become somewhat wrapped up in themselves, their issues, and their adventures.

When Crystal arrived, in spite of her commanding stature and presence, she had a calm and appreciative spirit. She hobbled into my office on her hurt foot and explained to me the issue she was having with her pack. I immediately liked her.

She had some kind of brain implants with leads that ended just above her collarbone. The batteries to keep that system working had been surgically inserted into her lower back. The problem was this: the shoulder straps of her pack rubbed against the leads on her collarbone, and the waist strap abraded where the battery pack was nestled. Some people had already tried to help her by adding extra padding to the areas that were sore. None of it had helped.

I love an engineering puzzle, and this was a fabulous one. In his book *Subtract*, Leidy Klotz demonstrates how we often neglect a basic way to improve a situation. We are quick to come up with things to add (like additional padding) to solve a problem, but we often fail to consider what we could *subtract* to make things better.[11]

Based on Crystal's physical situation, adding additional padding, no matter how soft, wasn't fixing the problem. There was still weight to be distributed, and the areas of her leads were just too sensitive, despite her indomitable spirit to power through. We needed a different approach.

"What if we were to remove some of the padding from those areas and build up extra padding adjacent to them, to build a kind of bridge across the tender portions and eliminate pressure?" I suggested.

Her face lit up.

We crafted a quick proof of concept with some pieces of foam I had lying around.

"I think it'll work!" she said. "It's a brilliant solution."

Since she was next heading back to Minnesota because of her foot, leaving off her attempt until next year, Crystal left her pack with me to adjust.

This was where other people came into play. Remember when I was first trying to get my Gossamer Gear packs manufactured and I found a cut-and-sew operation that could help me? That was Kay and Kim, the two sisters who ran Quest Outfitters. We had stayed in touch.

I sketched out how I was going to adjust Crystal's pack and contacted the sisters to source the foam I'd need.

I sent an email: "I'm looking for some foam that is about ¾ inch thick . Do you have any leads on something like that? I notice yours is only ⅜ inch thick, but I thought you might have an idea on where I could get some ¾ inch-thick stuff."

Kay wrote back right away and helped me figure out how to do this adjustment.

"We do not have ¾ inch but you could use a spray adhesive (the kind that is used for car headliners works great but really any spray foam should work) and just glue two ⅜ inch- to make a ¾ inch-thick piece. The foam we carry is pretty dense but does have a little bit of sponginess. We have some slight 2nds in the foam (mostly 2nds because they have some minor scratches on them, still very usable). If that might work for your experimenting, I can send that along to you at no charge. Just let me know how we can help or if you have any other questions. Glad you are still out there inventing and problem solving."

I was so touched by their generosity, offering to send the materials at no charge, and wrote back to tell them so. The response I got to that email was remarkable.

"It is the least we can do for you; you have been a great customer over the years and not to mention the G4. People still love that pack, and it has encouraged a lot of people over the years to make their own gear, which was one of our business goals."

All these years we'd worked together, I hadn't realized that one of their goals had been to encourage more people to make their own gear. It turns out that when I put up the sewing instructions for the G4, I'd inadvertently played a part in the success of the DIY portion of their business. It was so satisfying to hear them tell me that.

And true to their word, the foam soon arrived. I was able to adjust the pack, and Crystal Gail Welcome was soon back out on the trail, pioneering increased representation in the wilderness for BIPOC and disabled hikers like her.

But I also want to point out something that often gets overlooked with these kinds of feel-good stories, and that's that life doesn't always feel good. A facet of being human is that occasionally sadness will come to us. I was particularly moved by Crystal Gail Welcome's recent internet posts on dealing with mental illness and being bipolar. The more we talk about these things, the more we see what we have in common, and hopefully, instead of separating ourselves from others and feeling either superior or inferior, we recognize that we all share the human condition in its myriad forms.

And one of those forms is sadness. I'm not talking about mental illness here or serious depression but the fact that grief and times of desolation will visit every one of us, and learning to see them as a gift rather than a curse can change our resistance.

In our culture, we seem very focused on the hunt for pleasure. It's baked into our very Declaration of Independence: "Life, liberty, and the pursuit of happiness." As such, we may come to believe that not being happy all the time is a personal failing. For anyone experiencing loss or dejection, the blues, and a feeling of "what does it mean, anyhow?" this incessant cultural focus on happiness can make us all feel terribly isolated. Perhaps as a culture, we've grown afraid of the idea of sadness, doing all in our powers to keep it from our doors. But I've learned that sadness is part of being human and it brings its own, albeit sometimes hard to recognize, gifts.

I was sad to the point of nearly breaking when Derek was born with his many challenges and when Francie became clinically depressed trying to care for him. There were many nights when it was almost too much to bear. Then years later, his death gutted me. Likewise, though my mother was prepared for and desiring to leave us, her departure left a stamp of loss and grief on my heart. This is the normal way humans process emotion.

LIFE DOESN'T ALWAYS FEEL GOOD. A FACET OF BEING HUMAN IS THAT OCCASIONALLY SADNESS WILL COME TO US.

Some people fear that if they allow sadness to appear, they're giving in to depression, but that's not at all true. We honor the people in our lives who are no longer present by missing them. It's a sign that we've loved deeply, that their leave-taking left a vacuum and filled us with sorrow. That's not a sign that we are weak emotionally; rather, it's proof that we're fully tuned into our lives as we're experiencing them. As the world continues to adjust to life after the pandemic that paralyzed much of normal human interactions and took so many loved ones, it's normal to feel sad about what we've all experienced, the opportunities that were missed, the people who suffered. To *not* do so strikes me as willfully resistant to what is real.

When I am as awake as possible to my life as it's unfolding, I will naturally feel all kinds of emotions, from joy and love and acceptance to what's termed the more "negative" emotions like sorrow, loss, grief, and anxiety. I may not want to welcome those emotions with the same kind of open arms I have for the positive ones, but still, they're the backbone of what allows me to feel the joy. Because what I've found is that to the same degree I allow myself to feel the lows, that's the height at which I'll be able to feel the joy.

When I feel sadness over, say, a relationship with a friend that went amiss, I learn from that pain. As a result, I will bring a new attention to the next friendship I find myself in. Grief at the loss of a loved one makes me pay more attention to and cherish more deeply those still in my life.

But when sadness gets to feel too heavy—and again, I'm not talking about clinical depression here—I've found a few ways to deal with it that work for me. One surefire way to navigate through sadness is to be of service to someone else. When I get out of myself and my personal bog of despondency by seeing what I can add to another's life, it works every time.

To be clear, I'm not advocating that we sidestep sadness and grief by acts of service. No. It's important to feel those emotions. And what works for me may be different than what works for you. But when the sadness starts to feel too heavy or continues on too long, it does my soul good to turn my attention away from my inner pain and look to the world around me. What can I do that might help someone else? A phone call to check on a friend? Taking a meal to someone who's housebound? Asking someone who's been going through a rough patch to take a walk? It doesn't have to be much.

Plus it provides us a new perspective on our own situation that allows us to see what we can still be grateful for.

So much of how we feel about ourselves and our lives is dependent on our perspective. Which side of the equation are we giving the most attention to? Which wolf are we choosing to feed? Because for me, happiness is not about a lack of hardship (every life includes hardship) but about perseverance and where I choose to focus.

Here's the truth: I can tell two very different stories about my life, and both are completely accurate.

This is the hardship story: I was a nervous, anxious kid. When my parents divorced in the middle of my fourth-grade year, I was distraught. I cried so much my parents had to move me into another room so my crying wouldn't keep my brother and sister awake. We left sunny Southern California with our mom to drive across the entire country in the middle of winter and ended up in an apartment in Amherst, Massachusetts. I had to start a new school where I knew no one. When I joined the Boy Scouts, I was sexually molested. And then when my mom took me for psychological counseling, that psychologist also abused me. I was not popular at school and didn't have many friends. After high school, I moved back to California, where I married Francie. When she was pregnant with our second child, I almost died in a plane crash that killed the pilot. Then Derek was born severely disabled, and the cost for medical insurance on my fledgling company went from $600 a month to $8,000. Then the economy tanked and my business went with it. I worked for a year with no pay and had to take out a second mortgage on the house to pay our staff until I was finally forced to shutter the business. Meanwhile, Francie's depression brought on by Derek's struggles spiraled out of control, all while I was working eighty-plus hours a week to keep the financial wheels on.

Sounds pretty grim, doesn't it? And if I focus on that grimness, I will miss all the happiness that takes place in story number two, which is also true.

This is the happiness story: I was a nervous, anxious kid. I was raised by intelligent, loving, and involved parents, who instilled good values and morals in me. When they divorced and my mother moved us across the country, thanks to family money, she was able to continue caring full time for us kids. We had amazing educational opportunities and lacked for nothing. Boy Scouts fostered in me a love of the outdoors that led to incredible successes later in life. In high school, I was the tri-captain of the lacrosse team and president of the Outing Club before I organized a forty-two-hundred-mile bicycle trip across the United States with three friends. Taking two years "off" school, I worked at an engineering firm and found my passion for civil engineering, which set me on my future career course. I graduated in four years summa cum laude and moved to San Diego with an amazing woman I met at my apartment complex and somehow convinced to marry me. I worked for local firms before starting out on my own and always had enough work. I used not just my engineering skills but marketing skills to build my company. When the economy tanked, I was able to find jobs elsewhere for all my employees before shuttering the business and going to work for another firm. The birth of our disabled son, Derek, brought me to Jesus, a huge turning point and strength in my life. Because of my involvement with Boy Scouts as a leader and giving back to my community, I started a backpacking company on the side. That turned into a multimillion-dollar business. Though I've never taken a salary from the company I formed, it gave me relationships all over the world with amazing people: Guinness World Record holders, National Geographic Explorers, renowned endurance athletes, A-list directors and actors—all of whom I count as friends. Today, Francie and I have control over our time and money and enjoy amazing freedom. We live in a custom home in a location we chose with scores of genuine friends as neighbors. What an amazing life!

Both stories are absolutely true. They just depend on where I put the focus. Which one are you focusing on?

If, as Mary Poppins said, "Enough is as good as a feast," then there comes a time when we've experienced the present sadness enough and it's time to shift the focus. Try it, or find out what helps *you* get outside of yourself.

LESSON 15

Say Yes

WHEN I THINK OF THE NATURAL HUMAN TENDENCY TO SHY AWAY from new and unknown experiences, I'm reminded of Aunt Neva, my father's sister. Growing up, it was just her and my father, both very logical and not very emotional. He became an engineer and she worked for the Federal Reserve as an economist, both very rational and logic-based professions. Aunt Neva was never one for idle chatter. If Francie and I made plans to visit her and to, say, meet for lunch, as soon as we'd put our forks down and dabbed our mouths with our napkins, she was done.

"Okay, that was great. See you later," and bam! she'd be out of there. She didn't want to hang around and chat. And not being great with small talk myself, I could definitely identify with some of that.

She once told Francie that it would not occur to her to have lunch with a person unless that person had information to impart to her or she had information to impart to them. The idea of companionship, of sharing a few laughs, of just having an experience together was simply not something she sought.

When she was younger, she'd traveled a bit and had been in Prague. She told her family about it when she got home.

"I saw Mr. Wilson, our neighbor from across the street, eating in a café in Prague as I walked past," she said.

"Oh. That's amazing! Did you go over and say hi?" her mother asked.

"No. Why would I?" she replied.

"Well, it's pretty wild to run into someone on the other side of the globe. Seems like a good opportunity to acknowledge that astonishment and to celebrate seeing a face from home."

"I wouldn't cross the road to say hi to him here, so why would I do that in Prague?"

I'm grateful that I've learned to see things a little differently. Yes, I'm still an engineer and that cut-and-dried mindset lurks within me, but I've learned there's much to be gained in simply hanging out with people, in saying yes sometimes to opportunities that present themselves. And since I've experienced so many delightful surprises along the way, that history encourages me to continue assenting to the unknown. Sure, though I feel that social anxiety many of us share in these situations, I can also talk myself down from my anxiety and stay present with the people and experiences around me. When I do that, I never know what's going to happen next.

In fact, a number of amazing things have happened in my life, the result of simply saying yes to whatever is on offer. Often, I don't know if I'm embarking on a good experience or a bad one from the outset, but I work hard not to see the world in those dualistic terms. Usually, I just tell myself that I'm simply going to have an experience of some sort and I can decide after the fact if I ever want to do that particular thing again. And while I acknowledge there's great power in the word *no* and knowing your limits, drawing your boundaries, knowing what you do and do not want to pull into your life, I know that for me, I am often tempted to say no simply out of a slight sense of discomfort. If something doesn't feel familiar, sometimes that's enough for us to turn our backs on it. But often, it's in those very moments of uneasiness that we discover the magic. Or at least, that's what I've found.

Back when Mike and I were pedaling our way through the Great Divide trip, for instance, we stopped one night at the Horse Prairie Stage Stop, a small café in Grant, Montana (population 19 per the 2020 census), for a well-deserved night of burgers and beers. We were hot and tired and grimy, and it felt marvelous to be in an air-conditioned space, our hands wrapped around a hot-off-the-grill bun, an ice-cold brew within arm's reach, none of it covered in dust and sand and organic debris.

A pretty young woman was serving us and wanted to hear about our trek. Her name was Amelia, and throughout the evening she learned a bit about us and we learned a bit about her. The manager had introduced Amelia as the future Miss Montana, which Amelia quickly corrected, specifying that she had applied, but there was a lot of competition.

How many Miss Montanas have you met? To us, she was something special, even if she hadn't claimed the crown. Having someone excited to hear about all the places we were riding made the hours pass pleasantly. As the night wore down and we prepared to leave, she gave us an inside tip.

"The road you're taking tomorrow will be through this ranch where I do some work," she said. "It'll take you pretty much the whole day to make it through; that ranch goes on and on and on. So when you see a bunkhouse, go to the door and knock. Tell them Amelia sent you and that you want to take a shower. They'll take care of you."

We thanked her for her kindness and left to make our beds for the night out back under the stars.

The next day, we hit the road again, Amelia's offer far from our consciousness, our feet going round and round on the pedals, the smell of alfalfa in our noses. Before we knew it, we found ourselves riding through the massive cattle ranch she'd mentioned. Was she a cook there? A server? The rancher's daughter?

The size of the ranch was so massive, I wondered how the ranchers knew that they'd have enough hay for the coming winter. When I saw one of the ranchers working, I stopped riding to ask him about it. I was curious as to how they plan such things, and though I might have been tempted to keep the question to myself and to mind my own business, allowing my instinctual introvert tendencies to take over, I vanquished that inclination and reminded myself that people like to share about the things they know well. The man might very well be pleased as punch to answer my queries, glad to contribute his hard-won knowledge. Sure enough, as soon as I asked him how they knew how much hay they'd need, he was off on a tear.

I WAS FASCINATED BY ALL THIS; I LOVE UNDERSTANDING HOW PEOPLE DO ALL KINDS OF JOBS I KNOW NOTHING ABOUT.

"Well, you know, we have ten thousand head of cattle, and cattle, in general, eat about twenty-four pounds of hay a day. So it's just a little math, you know? The average round bale of hay has about twelve hundred and fifty pounds. Right now, we're a little behind on our haying. You can see we're cutting the field down here."

I was fascinated by all this, but I could tell that Mike, though he had stopped when I had approached the rancher, was now getting a bit bored with us geeking out on these details. But I love understanding how people do all kinds of jobs I know nothing about. Mike fidgeted and soon started riding on ahead. I figured I should get moving too.

As I was about to take off, the rancher added a final detail. "In fact, we're bringing some cattle down from the high pasture any minute now. They'll be coming down the road you're riding. When you see them, just pull over and they'll pass you by, no harm."

"Good to know," I called out as I hurried to catch up with Mike. "Thank you."

I told Mike what the rancher had said, and we biked on. We'd made it no more than a few miles farther before the most amazing thing happened. It felt like we had ridden onto a movie set for an epic Western. Sure enough, here came the cowboys with their dogs, herding what looked to be hundreds of cattle, ropes flying, dogs barking, horses whinnying, cattle lowing, and cowboys and cowgirls calling out commands. We pulled to one side as this tidal wave of life, like one huge moving organism, shifted around us. We felt as if, for these few minutes, we'd joined their movie and watched, rapt, filming what we could on our phones, our jaws down near our chests with awe.

Soon, though, most of the herd had passed us and Mike started to cycle on. I stayed behind to get some final pictures when a cowgirl on a horse rode up.

"Hey, Glen. Y'all get those showers?"

It was Amelia! After slinging burgers and beers last night, she'd changed into chaps and was now out here wrangling steers, dogies, and critters on the high plains with these other cowpokes. Could life be any more amazing? If I hadn't stopped to speak to the rancher, might we have missed this spectacle?

Later during the trip, on a rest evening, Mike and I checked into a little motel for a shower and a proper night's sleep. We paid a few bucks to stream the Miss Montana competition and root for Amelia. We learned even more about her, from the beautiful evening gown she had sewn herself to her volunteer efforts to end the epidemic of endangered and missing Indigenous women and girls. After watching the entire competition, we were distressed when she didn't win the crown; we both agreed that she'd been robbed. She was beautiful, talented, and a professional cowgirl to boot!

Man, she cleaned up nice, but I have to say, her facility on that horse was what won us over. Mike and I were quite sure the lovely young woman who won the crown that night couldn't hold a candle to Amelia on a horse.

But that's the beauty of life and the people we meet each day. Who knows when Miss Montana—okay, Miss Montana runner-up, but for Mike and me, she'll always be Miss Montana—is going to ride up on a horse in the middle of a cattle drive. You never know who you're going to meet unless you say yes when opportunity comes along.

For many thru-hikers, this kind of mystical synchronicity is sometimes referred to as trail magic, the amazing things that happen when you're out and about, when you open yourself to new experiences, when you pay attention.

One of the most amazing trail magic moments happened for me when I was backpacking with our youngest son, Grant, in 2002. On our final day we were hiking down a section of the PCT that's all desert scrub and hot, like you're walking through an oven. Neither one of us was having a blast, but we were getting close to being back home, and just being out in the wild together with my son was satisfaction galore, even if it wasn't the most beautiful day and the conditions were pretty blistering and uncomfortable. Just a few more miles, I kept telling him. He was a good sport and kept moving forward. After a while, he got a few paces ahead of me. Out of nowhere, he called out, alarm in his voice.

"Dad! What's this?"

I caught up with him and he pointed to the dirt, where etched into the hard-baked ground were letters, a message. An arrow pointed to one side and the letters spelled out my first name.

Huh? "I have no idea," I said to Grant, "but let's check it out."

We looked in the direction of the arrow, and there was a little bush that created a minor patch of shade in this scorching desert region, and underneath it, two cans of Coca-Cola, looking for all the world like the mirage they must be. How in the world had this happened? I picked one of the cans up. It was ice cold. I handed it to Grant.

"What did you do, Dad? How did you set this up? Pizza last night was great, but this..."

He opened his can, and I took the other. I wanted to take credit, but frankly I had no idea how this delightful treat had gotten here and why. Maybe there was another Glen hiking through? I hoped we hadn't usurped his drinks. The first few glugs of the Coke were heavenly. After days in the wilderness and in these dry and desiccated conditions, it tasted like ambrosia of the gods.

"This, Grant, is what we call 'trail magic.'"

"How did it get here?"

"I don't know. That's why it's called magic. But I'm certain there's an explanation."

Sure enough, there was. By the end of that day, we got to the trailhead and ran into a friend whose trail name is Azabat. Turns out he'd seen my post on Facebook that I was doing this hike with my son. Azabat was a hardcore hiker himself and had figured out a way to hike this section of the trail with his own mini-shuttle service. He had a little pickup truck that he used to tow his VW bug behind. He'd leave one vehicle at the end of the trail and then drive himself back to the beginning to hike it. He also knew the trail very well and, in fact, knew that in the place where he'd left the Cokes, the fire road he used for his shuttle was only a short distance away, like fifty feet, though we never saw it or knew it was there. He'd stopped and etched the sign in the dirt, leaving the Cokes for us, knowing he'd absolutely delight us and also make a fabulous story.

Once he'd explained all that, he drove us in his car to a little store down the road for ice cream sandwiches. Grant was blown away and to this day thinks I have a way of calling forth amazing things. Let's not tell him differently, okay?

But even Grant's eventual career choice, I can see now, was the result of the magic that happens when we say yes to whatever shows up. As a kid, only five or six years old, he was really fixated on his favorite pieces of clothing. At this one stage, it was a particular pair of underwear he adored. He wore those things so often that they finally ripped. He was distraught.

"Hey, Mom. Can you fix these?" he asked Francie.

"Sure, Grant. Just put it in my sewing room."

But Francie was busy and didn't get to fixing the underwear as quickly as Grant would have liked. I mean, come on, she was raising three kids and keeping house for all of us. His favorite underwear wasn't her top priority right then. But as she walked by that sewing room a few days later, there was Grant, hunched over her sewing machine. He'd figured it all out. She'd had lime green thread on the bobbin because she'd been doing some embroidery, but that hadn't stopped Grant. He managed to repair his favorite underwear on his own with that lime green thread, and before we knew it, he was at work, designing and making garments of his own. He's now a fashion designer, with his own brand, Towndust. This is what saying yes looks like in practice.

That same attitude helped Francie and me when we first made plans to move from San Diego to Bend in 2018. Even before we built our house in Oregon, we knew the neighborhood we wanted. We were walking around it one day, trying to decide if we'd buy a lot and build or if we'd find an already constructed house that might work for us.

As we walked and talked, we met someone, and because I said hi and made conversation rather than giving in to my introverted self, we were invited later in the year to a neighborhood Christmas party. Of course, we said yes to the invite.

The minute we were at the party, Francie and I split up to circulate, taking mental notes on the people we met. Soon, we both had lists of people we'd found who seemed fun and interesting, an entire registry of future potential friends before we even broke ground on our new home. And sure enough, our instincts were spot-on. Many of our dear friends in Bend we first identified at that party.

That circle of friendship continued to grow.

We built our house and then moved in. I was working on one of my tent designs and needed to test it out. Alas, because so many hours of my life had been taken up mowing and trimming our yard in San Diego, we'd planned our new house with all pavers, no lawn at all. I was thrilled to no longer be doing lawn maintenance, but how was I going to test my tent?

I went to my neighbor to ask if I could sleep in his backyard. What do you know, we're now good buddies!

Meanwhile, Francie, who isn't a big hey-let's-sleep-on-the-ground-tonight kind of person, came up with an idea: we should get a camper van. Initially, I was opposed because it seemed the opposite of my "take less" ethos (my exact words were "no good can come of this"), but I loved spending time with Francie. If we did this, we could take more trips together.

Eventually, we got one and named it Wally. Now we spend even more time together, doing something we both enjoy. And while Wally is not as minimal as my normal backpacking setup, he *is* pretty minimal compared to the huge Class A motorhomes we see. He fits in a standard parking stall, and with four-wheel drive and upgraded suspension, he can get deep into the woods where Francie can have her fluffy bed and I can have nature surrounding us.

There's always a new adventure if we stay open to them. That's the secret, at least in my book. Stay open and willing to say yes.

Conclusion

FRANCIE AND I ARE WALKING THE PATHS OF BEND, PART OF OUR plan for getting in shape for a long trek we're preparing to do in Europe this summer, a seven-hundred-kilometer hut-to-hut trip along the Alpe Adria Trail, traveling from Austria, through Slovenia, arriving in Italy—yet another harebrained idea we've said yes to.

The snows have mostly melted and bulbs are popping their head through the soil almost everywhere we look. The air smells of pine needles warmed by the spring sun, and the day couldn't be more beautiful. We take in the amazing birdsong as we walk, from the melody of the American robin to the high-pitched song of the yellow warbler. I especially love hearing the mountain chickadee, whose cheerful call carries a distance as the small, active birds flit from tree to tree. I can hear the spotted towhee scratch through leaves on the ground in search of food, even when it's not emitting its distinctive "drink-your-tea" call. And the most magnificent of all, the red-winged blackbird with its red-and-yellow wing patches, takes my breath away as it sings from the top of cattails and other tall vegetation near water sources.

After a short time, we find ourselves along a path maybe a mile from our house, enjoying the day. A few yards in front of us, a runner has stopped her workout and is trying to coax a terrified dog of an indeterminate compact breed, clearly one who's gotten away from its owners or is lost. The dog is old, with fogged eyes, wearing a harness but no tag. He's a little skittish. Francie and I approach, hoping to help. The dog will approach us, but he won't let any of us grab him.

"I think it's a stray," the runner says. "I don't know what to do about it, but I can't just leave it out here."

"We passed a gym a little ways back," I say. "I'll run back there and see if they have a leash or something we can use."

When I return a few minutes later with a leash, Megan the runner is able to get it on the dog.

"Maybe he's hungry," I suggest. "We can take him and backtrack to Sparrow Bakery HQ and get him a piece of bread or something, then take him to the humane society."

"You'd be okay with him? Thank you! Let me get your number so I can follow up and see how this all turns out," Megan says.

I give her one of my Gossamer Gear business cards.

At Sparrow, I approach Tara, one of the workers who knows me from my dishwashing shifts. "Do you have some leftover bread or something we can feed this stray dog we're trying to care for? We need to get him to the humane society, but I think he might be hungry."

Tara comes out to look at the dog and examines him like a pro. Turns out, she volunteers at a local vet clinic. "I'll be right back," she says, then reappears a minute later with a handful of ham slices for the sweet dog.

The dog thinks that stuff is pretty tasty, and now his ordeal doesn't seem quite as harrowing as it did earlier. I snap a photo of the dog and upload it to NextDoor in case his owner is looking for him or someone recognizes him. As the minutes pass, though, no response.

Francie and I take the dog home with us because it's still early in the morning and the humane society doesn't open until ten. I call at ten to double-check that they are indeed open and am preparing to take the dog there when I get a message on Nextdoor.

A woman named Julia says the dog belongs to her coworker; he's been looking for him for the last two hours. Soon, Jake comes over to collect the dog. Sammy is overjoyed to see his dad and can't contain his excitement. While Jake pets the dog and recounts his ordeal and frantic attempts to find Sammy, I learn that Jake is a surveyor working at AKS Engineering, whose offices are actually right across the parking lot from Sparrow HQ. I have seen that business countless times and for years harbored the idea of popping in to see if they ever needed an extra body every now and again. But I have never gotten around to actually doing it. I mention this to Jake.

He gives me the card for the head of that office. "We're having a big company meeting right now," he says, "and I need to get back, but we should connect again later." We make plans to do so.

Next, I hear back from Megan, the runner. When she got home, she'd told her partner, Matt, about the stray dog and shared with him my card.

"I was *just* on the Gossamer site last night, looking for new gear for you after our last backpacking trip to Goat Rocks! That guy lives in Bend?" Matt said. Turns out Matt is an engineer like me.

The coincidences continue. Over time, we get to know Megan, who happens to be Megan Marie Myers, a very successful local artist, turning forty next year and wanting to do a big trip. So in no time, she comes over and spends a couple of hours trying on packs and picking up tips, food samples, and so on. We're going to have her and Matt over for dinner when we get back from Europe. Megan is thinking she wants to do a hut hike next year and is anxious to pick our brains and see some photos from our trip. Meanwhile, though, she'll help Francie with getting a business started. Megan has contacts for getting Francie's handmade sewn and embroidered cards scanned and printed so she can set up a little shop on Etsy. Francie just gives away her cards, even though she spends hundreds of hours making them, but sometimes people want cards in a larger quantity than she can make. She's thinking if she could scan and print some of her favorite designs, they wouldn't be as special as her handsewn ones, but she could sell them inexpensively on Etsy to give people that option.

Megan is super fun, and I think the four of us are going to end up good friends. So one dog escaping provided introductions to help Francie with her cards, to help Megan and Matt with their gear needs, to help Megan with intel on hut hiking, and to connect me to possible part-time engineering/surveying work. This is the amazing world we live in. On the surface, it might look like just a slew of happy accidents, but I've heard that coincidences are simply miracles where God wishes to stay anonymous. I like to think that.

When we return from Europe, I go back to work at Sparrow—gotta keep my dishwashing chops in tip-top shape!—and appreciate this job more than I ever thought I would. I love all the interactions with young people and the way I'm getting to know more folks in my town. It's funny how many people I've come to know, because, at heart, I'm really quite shy. That's the beauty of having this job: it gives me a reason to have conversations, to see and be seen, to get out of my shell a bit. If I had thought this job was beneath me, I would have missed out on so much.

Because of it, I befriended the local TV weatherman, and this led to seeing my tie collection given new life on the evening newscast. Francie and I love watching the evening broadcast to see which of my old ties is making a cameo that night. Each time I see one, I remember wearing it for important occasions in my own work life, and it gives me a moment to reflect and be nostalgic. I love when physical objects that had once been important to me become touchstones for someone else.

Also, to help more of our neighbors get to know each other, Francie and I initiated Growler Thursdays. We invite anyone who's around to come on over. We provide pretzels and mixed nuts, plus a great patio for hanging out, and others bring whatever they want to drink. It's become a weekly gathering, and our neighbors have made so many new connections, simply by our throwing our doors wide open. One neighbor now refers to me as "the mayor of Lolo Drive"— an unexpected outcome for a shy kid who worried he'd never find his way in life.

I also recently reconnected with someone who used to work for me when I was employed by the city of Carlsbad. She was looking for a patent attorney and then a product designer for a side project she was working on. Thanks to all the people I've gotten to know, I was able to hook her up. Another friend wanted to sell his website. He benefited from a friend-of-a-friend I put him in contact with who was able to help.

When you're ultralight backpacking, you meet people and have the opportunity as you walk along to move beyond surface conversations. Often, you find yourself either helping someone else or receiving help. Because you carry so little with you, such interactions are unavoidable. But that's the beauty of it, and it's what I strive to bring into my daily life. By taking less, I'm able to do more, and the result benefits the entire community. What more could we want for a healthy and fulfilling life?

What are the ways this philosophy of "take less, do more" might benefit your life? What's stopping you? If one of these lessons appeals, maybe start there and see where the path leads. Then try a second one. Many amazing experiences are just waiting for you around the next bend.

Appendix

For downloadable sample gear lists, helpful tips, videos, and more, visit www.GlenVanPeski.com/resources

You can find the G4 instructions as mentioned in Lesson 10 at www.glenvanpeski.com/tips_advice/ultralight-pack

Sample Gear Lists
Bridge of the Gods to White Pass, First Leg, August 2020
Length/Distance: 51 miles; 3 days (first leg)
Weather: sunny, highs around 80°F, lows to 40°F

Item	Description / Notes /Rationale	in pack 4.61	wear / carry 4.71	consume 5.96	max. on back 10.56
PACK - SHELTER - SLEEPING					
backpack	GG Murmur - no belt	7.8			
waterproof pack cover	Mylar bag	1.0			
sleeping pad	GG Thinlight 3/8" - 30" l, 12-16" w	2.1			
insulation pad	none	0.0			
shelter	GG Whisper (prototype)	6.4			
shelter support (poles, etc.)	(Using trekking poles)	0.0			
shelter stow sack	None	0.0			
stakes	1 Ti V-stake, 6 Easton FMJ	1.6			
stake bag	None	0.0			
guylines	Included in shelter weight	0.0			
sleeping bag (no stuff sack)	GG Sleeplight long	17.2			

Item	Description / Notes /Rationale	in pack 4.61	wear / carry 4.71	consume 5.96	max. on back 10.56
ground sheet or bivy sack	GG Polycryo small	1.0			
CLOTHING					
underwear - bottoms	Ex Officio Sport briefs		2.6		
base / wicking layer top	Columbia PFG nylon long sleeved		8.9		
base / wicking layer bottom	REI convertibles (tall)		13.2		
insulating top	Montbell Ex Light down jacket L	5.7			
insulating bottoms	Patagonia Capiline	0.0			
raingear (hard shell) top	Berghaus Hyper Jacket XL	3.2			
raingear (hard shell) bottoms	Zpacks CloudKilt	1.9			
waterproof glove shells	Outdoor Research	0.0			
windgear (soft shell) top	Mtn Hardware Ghost Whisperer Anorak	0.0			
camp shoes	medical booties	0.7			
warm gloves	Icebreaker wool	0.9			
warm hat	Zpacks fleece	1.0			
sun hat	Tilley		3.3		
sun gloves	Palm Free	0.0			
neck protection	Bandanna		0.9		
socks	Wright double-layer		1.3		
spare socks	Thin nylon	1.0			
gaiters	Simblissity Levagaiters		1.9		
sleeping socks	Fleece	1.8			
shoes	Altra Lone Peak RSM		25.4		
clothing stuff sack	Cuben fiber (Zpacks)	0.3			
COOKING - WATER					
stove	None	0.0			
windscreen	None	0.0			
fuel bottle	None	0.0			
matches / lighter	None	0.0			
cook pot	Amazon bubble envelope	0.8			
cook pot lid	None	0.0			
cook kit stuff sack	None	0.0			
utensils	GG long bamboo spoon	0.5			
food storage bag	homemade spinnaker	0.6			
bear bag hang system	Aloksak	0.0			
bear bag hang system	60' spectra 725 line, garlic bag, mini carabiner	0.0			
water storage	1 l Smart Water bottle	1.6			

Item	Description / Notes /Rationale	in pack 4.61	wear / carry 4.71	consume 5.96	max. on back 10.56
water storage	2+ liter Platy	1.5			
water storage	1 liter Platy	0.0			
water storage	Platy drinking tube	2.7			
water storage	2.5 gal container	0.0			
water treatment	NaClO in mini dropper bottle	0.4			
MISCELLANEOUS ITEMS					
signalling	whistle on lanyard		0.2		
headlamp	Petzl Bindi	1.2			
group light	LuminAID	0.0			
blade	Mini snips (carried on lanyard)		0.2		
trekking poles	GG Lightrek 5 no straps		9.2		
headnet	petersheadnets.com	0.5			
bug dope	Sawyer Maxi DEET spray	0.9			
sun	mini tube spf 30 plus mini lip balm	0.7			
toothbrush	GG Finger toothbrush and floss	0.2			
toothpaste	(use Dr. Bronner's)	0.0			
hygiene	Dr. Bronner's soap	0.2		0.1	
toilet paper	1/2 disposable shop towel per day	0.6			
hygiene	micro bottle alcohol gel	0.1		0.2	
LNT kit	WAG bag	0.0			
small items bag	Cuben fiber (Zpacks)	0.1			
blister & minor wound care	antibiotic, Band-Aids, compeed, etc	0.9			
meds	Imodium,Tums,Tylenol PM,naproxin, etc	0.8		1.0	
tweezers		0.1			
notes	Rite in the Rain page, Sharpie	0.4			
reading glasses	i4u lenses	0.2			
firestarting kit	Sparker and tinder	0.2			
repair	8" duct tape, needle/thread, safety pin	0.2			
sunglasses	Maui Jim prescription		0.7		
watch	Suunto CORE		2.4		
compass	(on watch)	0.0			
documentation	iPhone8		5.2		
emergency	Garmin InReach Mini	3.4			
battery	RavPower 6700 mA	0.0			
maps and permits		1.3			

Item	Description / Notes /Rationale	in pack 4.61	wear / carry 4.71	consume 5.96	max. on back 10.56
CONSUMABLES					
food - snacks	2.6 days at 1.4 lbs. per day			58.0	
water	1 L average carried			32.0	
fuel (Baro Cook)	2.0 oz. per day (hot dinners only)	0.0		4.0	

Great Divide Mountain Bike Route, July 2021

Length/Distance: 950 miles; 30 Days
Weather: high of 75°F, low around 45°F

Item	Description / Notes /Rationale	packed (g) 16904	worn (g) 2173	consumed (g) 3906	max. packed 20810
BIKE - PACKS		**12475**			
bike	Knolly Cache Titanium XL	10310			
seat bag	Revelate Terrapin	624			
handlebar bag	Salsa EXP Anything Cradle+top load bag	670			
handlebar top bag	Salsa EXP Front Pouch	150			
top tube bag	Salsa	117			
water bottle holders (2)	Revelate Mountain Feedbag	210			
frame bag	GG Custom	194			
down tube bag	Revelate Joey	129			
fork cage straps	Voile	40			
overlow capacity	Sea to Summit Nano pack	31			
SHELTER - SLEEPING		**1046**			
sleeping pad	GG ³/₈" Thinlight ³/₈" - 30" l, 12–16" w	62			
shelter	GG Whisper tent (prototype)	175			
shelter support	Easton Syclone Max 51" + 24"	144			
stakes	2 Ti V, 3 Easton FMJ (2 chopstakes)	40			
sleeping bag (no stuff sack)	GG Sleeplight Plus long	580			
ground sheet	GG Polycryo medium	45			
CLOTHING		**1111**	**1901**		
underwear - bottoms	Padded bike briefs	88	128		
underwear - when not riding	Y-Athletics	82			
base / wicking layer top	KUIU Ultra Merino 145 zip-T		220		
base / wicking layer top (town shirt)	Zoic	142			
base / wicking layer bottom	Eddie Bauer Guide convertibles	168	303		
insulating top	Montbell Plasma down jacket L	145			
insulating bottoms	none	0			
raingear (hard shell) top	Marmot Bantamweight	158			
raingear (hard shell) bottoms	Zpacks rain pants	86			
waterproof glove shells	Zpacks	24			
camp shoes	Clean room booties	44			
warm gloves	Possumdown	41			
warm hat	Zpacks fleece	31			
sun hat	GG running hat		59		

Item	Description / Notes /Rationale	packed (g) 16904	worn (g) 2173	consumed (g) 3906	max. packed 20810
gloves	Bike gloves		70		
helmet	Oakley bike helmet		304		
neck protection	Bandanna		19		
socks	Ultimax / Darned Tough	36	47		
sleeping socks	Fleece	51			
shoes	Altra Lone Peak 4 RSM		720		
gaiters	Altra		31		
clothing stuff sack	GG	15			
COOKING - WATER		370		4	
stove	TD gram cracker, screen, Ti simmer	6			
windscreen	TD Caldera Ti	25			
matches / lighter	paper matches + Wetfire	9		4	
cook pot	Zelph	20			
cook pot lid	Zelph	5			
cook kit stuff sack	GG insulated DCF	11			
utensils	GG Chopstakes® (prototype)	30			
food storage bag	homemade spinnaker	16			
bear bag hang system	Aloksak	35			
bear bag hang system	60' spectra 725 line, garlic bag, 2 biners	42			
water storage	2 – 1 l Arrowhead bottles w/ sport top	50			
water storage	2+ liter Platy	35			
water storage	Sawyer 1-liter	37			
water treatment	Sawyer Mini filter	40			
water treatment (backup)	mini dropper bottle bleach	9			
MISCELLANEOUS ITEMS		536	56	207	
signalling	whistle on lanyard		7		
blade	Mini snips (carried on lanyard)		5		
blade	Dermasafe		8		
headnet	petersheadnets.com	15			
bug dope	Sawyer Maxi Deet	26			
sun	mini tube spf 30 plus mini lip balm	22			
toothbrush	Travel toothbrush and floss	36			
toothpaste	(use Dr. Bronner's)	0			
hygiene	Dr. Bronner's soap	5		10	
toilet paper	1/2 disp. shop towel + Wet Wipe per day			20	
hygiene	bottle alcohol gel			32	

Item	Description / Notes /Rationale	packed (g) 16904	worn (g) 2173	consumed (g) 3906	max. packed 20810
small items bag	Smellly Proof pleated (2)	14			
blister & minor wound care	antibiotic, Band-Aids, compeed, etc	26			
meds	Imodium,Tums,Tylenol PM,naproxin, etc	23		1	
prescription + vitamins				98	
butt paste				29	
tweezers + tick remover		5			
lotion	Travel size			17	
notes (sketching)	Sharpie + mini notebook	32			
reading glasses	i4u lenses	7			
firestarting kit	Sparker and tinder	7			
repair	8" duct tape, needle/thread, safety pin	7			
bear spray	Counter Assault	301			
sunglasses	Tifosi		11		
sunglass case	fabric	10			
wallet	Nomatic		17		
rearview mirror for glasses			8		
maps	on phone	0			
ELECTRONICS		**469**	**216**		
watch	Suunto CORE		68		
compass	(on watch)	0			
camera/documentation	iPhone8		148		
emergency	Garmin InReach Mini	96			
battery	NiteCore 10,000 mAh	142			
cable with adapters		14			
charger plug		42			
notes	Sony ICD-TX800 voice recorder	22			
headlamp	NiteCore	32			
SRAM charger dock		31			
rear blinking light		81			
bag for small electronics	GG DCF	9			
TOOLS AND PARTS		**897**			
pump	EDC One pump with tools and CO2	320			
lock	Otto-lock 60"	266			
spare spokes + nipples		39			
spare valve cores		4			
tire plugs	Dynaplug	109			

Item	Description / Notes /Rationale	packed (g) 16904	worn (g) 2173	consumed (g) 3906	max. packed 20810
tire irons	Pedros	42			
valve/spoke tool	Park Tools VC-1	8			
electical tape		19			
disc brake spreader		5			
multi-tool	Fabric	85			
chain lube		52			
chain rag in ziploc		39			
tubeless tire fill		145			
toothbrush for chain cleaning		20			
bike rag		40			
CONSUMABLES				3695	
food - snacks	2.6 days at 1.4 lbs. per day			1650	
water	2 L average carried			2000	
fuel (Bluet fuel tabs)	15 g. per day (hot breakfast + dinner)			45	

First Aid Kit
Glen's First Aid and Repair/Emergency Kit
Revised August 30, 2019

Description	Use	in pack (oz.)	consume (oz.)	Total
Wound Care				
Omnifix - 7"	blister prevention	0.10		
Kinesio tape - 2"	blister prevention	0.03		
Compeed medium - 2	blister prevention	0.22		
Band-Aid medium adhesive strip	wound care	0.03		
ChitoSAM	hemostatic dressing	0.21		
Wound closures - 5	wound care	0.03		
Tagaderm Film - 2	wound coverage	0.17		
Bacitracin ointment - foil packet	antibacterial	0.05		
Hydrocortisone 1% - foil packet	anti-itch	0.05		
Burn gel	burn treatment	0.04		
Mini tweezer	splinters, ticks	0.02		
mini Ziploc	for opened ointment packs	0.01		
Smelly Proof 3 x 4	organization - bandages	0.10		
Subtotal blister and wound care		**1.06**		**1.06**
Medications				
Benadryl - 2 25 mg tabs (2 packets)	allergy	0.08		
Immodium - 2 doses in foil pkgs	anti-diarrheal	0.05		
Tums - 3 tabs in mini ziploc	stomach upset	0.29		
Gas-X - 1 strip	stomach upset	0.04		
Valtrex - 4 tabs in mini ziploc	prescription meds for fever blisters	0.22		
Excedrin - 6 caps in mini ziploc	altitude headaches		0.15	
Aspirin - 2 tabs in foil packet	heart	0.04		
Tylenol PM - 12 tabs in mini ziploc	thin sleeping pad equalizer		0.36	
Subtotal medications		**0.72**	**0.51**	**1.23**

Description	Use	in pack (oz.)	consume (oz.)	Total
Smelly Proof 4 x 6 case for first aid and repair/emergency		0.17		
Total First Aid		**1.95**	**0.51**	**2.46**
Repair/Emergency				
Krazy Glue mini	emergency repair, also wound closure	0.09		
Sparker	emergency fire starting	0.19		
Tinder	emergency fire starting	0.02		
Smelly Proof 3 x 3	extra waterproofing for fire starting	0.06		
SOL mini mirror	emergency signalling, tick checks	0.30		
Needle and thread	emergency repair	0.01		
Safety pins (2)	emergency repair	0.03		
Duct tape - 6"	repair	0.10		
Tenatious Tape - 6"	repair	0.16		
Total Repair/Emergency		**0.96**		**0.96**

Acknowledgments

READ MILLER IS A MAN OF MANY IDEAS AND NOT QUITE AS MANY skills, at least in the DIY arena. The creation of the G4 pack, GVP Gear, and subsequently Gossamer Gear really stemmed from his ideas. Without Read's ideas and encouragement, I would have none of the adventures that have come from starting an ultralight gear company and the amazing circle of friends I have because of it.

Claire Bateman, my mom, felt strongly that every kid should leave home knowing how to cook, bake, and sew. Because I knew how to sew, I was able to put ideas into action and sew a lighter pack and other gear, which started me down an incredible journey.

Chris Van Peski, my dad, is also an engineer. He could always figure out the answer to any engineering problem I had in college and is also wise in figuring out life. He has been an inspiration in many ways and is still helping me solve problems today.

John Mackey saved Gossamer Gear when I didn't have the time or energy to continue it. But more than saving Gossamer Gear, as wonderful as that has been in my life, John's inclusion of me on trips with his group of amazingly interesting and talented friends has been an entrée into another world. Every trip with John and his family and friends is an advanced life seminar that always leaves me knowing things I didn't previously know and thinking about things I had not been thinking about. My life is infinitely richer for meeting John.

My wife, Francie, has shouldered the bulk of raising our boys while I ran an engineering company to (usually) pay the bills and a gear company for fun. She has gamely allowed scores of smelly hikers to sleep in our living room before they started the Pacific Crest Trail (PCT). She has worried as I left on backpacking trips, leaving her with the kids, including our severely handicapped middle son, Derek. Francie has supported my backpacking and related endeavors not because any benefits accrue to her but simply because she sees how much joy they bring me. She is both the toughest and most tenderhearted woman I know. Thank you for your love and support. I would not want to do life without you.

My sons Brian and Grant have both been backpacking with me. They grew up with an often absent dad due to the strains of running both an engineering practice and a backpacking company, and they seem to have made their peace with it. While Brian is more often found in the wilderness these days, they both have grown up to be strong entrepreneurs in their own right and kind, humble men that I am tremendously proud of.

Thank you to Bernadette Murphy, who helped bring my words and ideas together into a cohesive manuscript. Along the way, she has become a fast friend, we have backpacked together, and she has introduced me to other authors I would not otherwise have experienced without her. Without her professionalism, creativity, persistence, and agility, this book never would have come to fruition.

The team at Forefront Books pulled everything together into a book I'm proud of. Jonathan Merkh believed in the project when I had my doubts. The deft and intuitive hands of Michael Maudlin, the relentless detailed precision of Andrew Buss, and the vision and infectious enthusiasm of Jennifer Gingerich were instrumental in producing a solid, visually appealing book under tight deadlines, all under the watchful eye of the talented and supremely organized Jill Smith. Thank you all; I would not have wanted to produce my first book with anyone else!

Thanks to my friends who are successful authors and shared their insights about the process: Liz "Snorkel" Thomas, Heather "Anish" Anderson, Barney "Scout" Mann, Dan Buettner, Dr. Ben Michaelis, Mike Clelland, Lawton "Disco" Grinter, Dan Rockwell, Alexander Green, Ken Guidroz, Francis Tapon, Ali Selim, Patrick Gray, Henna Pryor, Scott McCain, Clint Greenleaf, Wayne Pacelle, Steve Boman, Kathy Dodson, Rohit Bhargava, Ryan Jordan—your comments were immensely helpful to a first-time author. Also thanks to those who served as beta readers, particularly: Julie Clark, Duncan Cheung, Jeff Van Peski, and Heather Pizzuto; the book is better because of your input.

I owe Becky Robinson and her team at Weaving Influence a huge debt for helping launch this book. Becky has been very generous in sharing her time and expertise about establishing an audience and expanding my reach.

I have learned so much about ultralight backpacking, and about life, from hundreds of people in my life. Many of your names appear in the book as part of the stories, but there are many more of you than there was room for stories. I'm eternally grateful that you're in my life, even if you're not in the book.

And finally, I want to acknowledge my God and my Savior Jesus Christ. Knowing him, and giving over my life to him, has made all the difference.

Notes

1 Wikiquote. "Antoine de Saint Exupéry." Accessed January 10, 2024. https://
   en.wikiquote.org/wiki/Antoine_de_Saint_Exup%C3%A9ry.

2 Kahneman, Daniel, and Angus Deaton. "High Income Improves Evaluation
   of Life but Not Emotional Well-Being." *Proceedings of the National Academy
   of Sciences* 107, no. 38 (September 7, 2010): 16489–93. https://doi
   .org/10.1073/pnas.1011492107.

3 Chicago Tribune. "Rich Think Big about Living Well," September 24, 1987.
   https://www.chicagotribune.com/news/ct-xpm-1987-09-24
   -8703120456-story.htmlhttps://www.chicagotribune.com/news/ct-xpm-
   1987-09-24-8703120456-story.html.

4 Epstein, David. "Happiness Is a 2x2 Matrix." *Range Widely*, March 24, 2023.
   https://davidepstein.substack.com/p/happiness-is-a-2x2-matrix.

5 Einhorn, Hillel. Interview with Hillel Einhorn for Open University,
   YouTube, uploaded March 24, 2023 by Emre Soyer https://youtu.be/
   W97UobO0UWs.

6 For more details, see Backpacking Light at https://backpackinglight.com/
   quick_healthy_meals_with_an_ultralight_cook_kit/.

7 This can be purchased from Gossamer Gear's website: www.gossamergear
   .com/collections/hydration-cooking/products/smelly-proof-stand-up
   -storage-bags.

8 Oxford Reference. "Thomas Alva Edison," n.d. https://doi.org/10.1093/
   acref/9780191826719.013.q-oro-ed4-00003960.

9 Carol S. Dweck, PhD, *Mindset: The New Psychology of Success* (New York:
   Random House, 2006).

10 See the fourteen-minute documentary made of her trek at https://
   bikepacking.com/plog/quinn-brett-tour-divide.

11 Klotz, Leidy. *Subtract.* Flatiron Books, 2021. http://books.google.ie/books
   ?id=_L_iDwAAQBAJ&printsec=frontcover&dq=Subtract:+The+
   Untapped+Science+of+Less&hl=&cd=5&source=gbs_api.